Rediscovering Mary

Rediscovering Mary

Insights from the Gospels

TINA BEATTIE

BURNS & OATES
Dove

An imprint of HarperCollins*Publishers*

First published in Great Britain 1995

Burns & Oates
Wellwood, North Farm Road
Tunbridge Wells, Kent TN2 3DR

Published in Australia as
A Dove publication
An imprint of HarperCollins*Religious*
(ACN 005 677 805)
A member of the HarperCollins*Publishers* (Australia) Pty Ltd group
22–24 Joseph Street
North Blackburn, Victoria 3130, Australia

ISBN 0 86012 247 6

Biblical extracts are from *The Jerusalem Bible* © 1966, 1967, 1968 by Darton,
Longman & Todd Limited and Doubleday & Company Inc., and are used by
permission.

National Library of Australia Cataloguing-in-Publication data:
Beattie, Tina, 1955–.
    Rediscovering Mary: insights from the Gospels.

    ISBN 1 86371 609 2.

    1. Mary, Blessed Virgin, Saint – History of doctrines.
    2. Mary, Blessed Virgin, Saint – Theology. 3. Bible –
    Feminist criticism. I. Title

232.91

ISBN (UK) 0 86012 247 6
ISBN (Australia) 1 86371 609 2

Typeset by Search Press Limited
Printed in Finland by Werner Söderström Oy

Contents

Beginning Again with Mary

It is widely believed today among Catholics as well as non-Catholics that Mary, the mother of Jesus, cannot serve as a source of inspiration for modern women. Defined and interpreted by celibate males, traditional Mariology has little to say about the challenges and aspirations of women in today's world. Priestly homilies delivered on Marian feast days are more likely to alienate and frustrate women in the congregation than to inspire them. It is hardly surprising that many choose to bypass Mary altogether, preferring such biblical figures as the sisters Martha and Mary, or Mary Magdalene, known as the "apostle to the apostles" in the early Church because she was the first to witness the Resurrection.

However, I believe Mary represents a tradition that, however tainted, constitutes the only abiding womanly presence in the history of the Christian Church. Although they are deeply flawed as they stand, in Mary the "feminine" values essential to the well-being of any society, and indeed to the spiritual and psychological health of any human being, have been kept alive in the Church. When these values are seen as the exclusive preserve of the female gender, leaving men free to develop "masculine" qualities of power and dominance, men and women become polarized from one another, and the just and loving community of God is turned into an arena where the battle to reinforce sexual stereotypes is waged beneath a flimsy veil of theological justification. Nobody reading the long history of Christian thought can fail to notice how much energy is expended on men trying to decide what to do about women, having transformed them into such alien and threatening feminine beings.

It is essential to salvage Mary and the values associated with her in a way that is relevant and liberating for all modern Christians, men and women, for without these values we surely cannot survive. To abdicate both the right and the responsibility to claim Mary as part of women's general reclamation of our Christian heritage is to practise a form of submission by yielding to the dominant interpretation rather than challenging it. We are all entitled to relate to Mary in ways that help us to deepen our faith and to express our humanity. She represents a rich resource for women's spirituality and for the rediscovery of the neglected elements of womanliness in the Church. This enterprise is of value for men as well as for women. In meeting Mary anew, men meet a part of themselves that they need to own. She offers men the opportunity to reclaim the motherly aspects of their own natures, just as she offers women the opportunity to reclaim their sense of autonomy and self-worth before God.

There are many ways of approaching Mary. We need only consider the difference between Mariology as defined and constrained by official Catholic doctrine, and the devotion to Mary that constitutes a fecund and often chaotic celebration of life expressed in festivals and liturgies throughout the Latin world. The history of Christian art reveals her to be the most adaptable and beloved of icons, appearing in many guises as an expression of the ways in which people have interpreted their faith through the ages. Nor is this a tradition that has been shaped and celebrated only by men. The work of women writers and mystics exhibits an enduring fascination with the Mother of God. Some doctrines, such as that of the Immaculate Conception, represent the Church's official endorsement of beliefs held by ordinary men and women for many centuries. The deconstruction of any tradition is a complex task, but with Mariology it is particularly difficult. The fact that a doctrine has been used in a manipulative or repressive way does not mean that it cannot nonetheless be true. It is surely more creative, and indeed incumbent upon Catholics, to engage with the Church's teaching in such a way as to discover its life-giving truth, than to throw the baby of revelation out with the bath water of ideology.

There has never been any shortage of books on Mary, but in recent years a new trend has become apparent. Tracts of pious devotion with a barely-concealed agenda aimed at keeping Catholic girls out of trouble no longer monopolize the popular market. Feminist theologians from the Third World have begun to write about Mary as a source of hope and inspiration for the poor. Western women too have begun to ask what Mary might mean for them, and there is a growing field of academic and popular literature that challenges traditional stereotypes. I have included some of these books in the bibliography, for readers who would like to know more about the theological and academic debates on the subject.

It is not my intention to write an academic book about Mary. My primary concern is to invite the ordinary reader to share some of my own joy at discovering the mother of Jesus relatively late in life, and finding in her a rich and surprising resource for my Christian faith. I converted to Catholicism in 1987 at the age of thirty-two. I had long felt attracted by Catholic spirituality, and while living in Zimbabwe in the early 1980s I became increasingly admiring of the Catholic Justice and Peace Commission's role in that country both before and after Independence, as a consistent and courageous defender of social justice. However, as an evangelical Christian I was deeply suspicious of "Mary worship," and Mariology was the great obstacle in the way of my becoming a Catholic. On one occasion at a Catholic faith enquiry evening, I was being shown around a church and the man leading our group pointed to a picture in a dim corner of the building, which I thought showed Mary breastfeeding Jesus. "That picture is called Our Lady with the Perpetual Sucker" he said, and I was outraged. It was only later when I told him how offensive I found it that Catholics should refer to Jesus as the Perpetual Sucker, that I discovered my mistake. It was of course a picture of Our Lady of Perpetual Succour. Eventually, I explained to the parish priest that although I felt a strong desire to become a Catholic, I could not participate in Catholic devotion to Mary. I was received into the Church in spite of this reservation, and I decided to remain open about what to do with Mary. Whereas Catholics were taught in childhood to come to Jesus through Mary, I decided that I would have to find a way to come to Mary through Jesus.

Looking back, there were a number of factors that eventually drew me to her. As a mother with very young children, accustomed to an evangelical church that perpetuated strong stereotypes about women and motherhood but lacked any religious symbols of motherhood, I began to identify with Mary as a mother. I decided to start praying the Rosary, as a way of becoming more familiar with Catholic devotion. As I meditated on the mysteries and read the scriptures about her, and as I familiarized myself with Catholic doctrine, I realized that there were dimensions to her that I had never explored but which increasingly had the power to sustain and inspire my own faith. I began to build up a picture of Mary, based on the Gospels and Catholic tradition, but also on my own experiences of womanhood and mothering. I moved to Bristol with my family in 1988 and did a degree in Theology and Religious Studies, and my interest in Mary grew as I read about her from the perspective of feminist and liberation theology. However, it should be said at the outset that I remain deeply antipathetic to much that is done in Mary's name in the Catholic Church, and I have never found myself attracted to traditional Catholic groups of Marian devotion. Perhaps it also needs to be pointed out that, unlike many Catholic women of my generation, I did not grow up in a church that used the Virgin Mary as a weapon against my own developing sexuality. It may be easier for a woman who has had a non-Catholic upbringing to enjoy and celebrate Mary than for a woman who has always been taught to see Mary as a rebuke to her own sexual desires.

Perhaps this abuse of doctrines concerning Mary results from a certain over-simplification, a tendency to hold her up as an impossible role model rather than to engage with her as a religious symbol rich in paradox. This is not to deny that there are aspects of Mary that can function as a role model for Christians, and I explore some of these in this book. The image of the *Theotokos*, the Great Mother of God, must not be allowed to obscure the humanity of Mary. It is only when Christian symbolism is rooted in the lives of the poor, in this case when the Mother of God is understood in the context of the poor Jewish girl of first-century Palestine, that it becomes redemptive. Any religion concerned only with the transcendent and the other-worldly is either boring or ethically suspect from a Christian point of view. Christianity is a religion of the body as well as of the spirit, worshipping the God whose Kingdom is on earth as well as in heaven. Sometimes, at different stages in our lives and in response to different needs, we may derive enormous comfort from identifying with Mary the Nazarene, the woman who shared in so many of the hopes and heartaches of women through the ages. But to reduce every aspect of Mary's life, including the profound mystery of her role as the Virgin Mother of God, to nothing more than an earthly example for good Christians to emulate, is to indulge in an inappropriate anthropomorphization of the Christian mystery. There are times when we need to respond to her as the Great Mother of God who is profoundly Other than us, who invites our spirits to leave behind all earthly realities and enter into the deepest mystery of God's love. In the Christ who is Jesus of Nazareth, in the *Theotokos* who is Mary of Nazareth, Christians experience both the immanence and the transcendence of God, the Kingdom of God that is and is to come.

The following reflections are based primarily on my own interpretation of the Gospel stories and I make no claims for their theological or exegetical credentials. While much excellent scholarly work is now being done in the field of feminist Mariology, I believe that there is a need for accessible books written for readers without theological expertise. Margaret Hebblethwaite writes that scripture is "there to be ours, to work with and play with and enjoy and explore."[1] This encapsulates the process I have brought to my readings about Mary. My evangelical background taught me to pay close attention to the biblical text, but whereas that used to mean that the Bible was a low ceiling on which I bumped my head every time I tried to leap too high, I now see it as a springboard from which the mind, the spirit and the imagination can launch themselves in an exhilarating leap toward the heavens. I have put aside the many interesting arguments of biblical criticism in order to allow the Gospels to speak for themselves. Legitimate though biblical criticism is, it would be a great loss if we denied ourselves the right to read the story of Christ as we might read great poetry, allowing ourselves to enter into the images and possibilities that are created and sensing the mysterious resonance of truth.

Those marginalized from the telling of history, including women, are learning to decipher the meaning of silence as well as of words, that silence which broods over so many historical texts and speaks eloquently of those who have been forbidden to speak. It is a silence that denotes the absence of voices which would tell different stories, ascribe different meanings to the world. In the interpretations men have given to the biblical texts about Mary, there is much of value and of insight, but the dominance of the

---

[1] Quoted in the *Journal of the Catholic Women's Network*, September 1994, p. 20

male perspective over the female means that there is also much that has been distorted and poorly understood. Despite the millions of words written about her, silence still surrounds Mary. The scriptures suggest that she had a tremendous quality of silence and contemplation about her, and they offer few biographical details. But the little we are told about her is pregnant with meaning, and as we begin to linger over the surface of the text we find ourselves being drawn in, seduced by the possibilities of language and of silence, by the subversive intention of the narrative which is possibly hidden even from the narrator.

I should say something about my use of language. Much of what I say about Mary is to do with the sin of patriarchy and the restoration of wholeness to the human condition. By a patriarchal society I mean one that favours a male understanding of life by silencing, subsuming or trivializing women's perspectives, and that enthrones masculine values of competitiveness, aggressiveness and domination, values that are usually but not always associated with men. Women in the rich West are often in a position of patriarchal power *vis-à-vis* men and women in poorer countries. A businesswoman might be the patriarchal oppressor of an unemployed man in her own community. Patriarchy is part of that flawed human inheritance we call original sin, the fundamental disordering of relationships which is a universal social malaise, a common feature of all societies and religions. While I think many feminist theologians fail to acknowledge the extent to which Christianity has challenged and overcome some of the more extreme aspects of patriarchy (for instance in the rejection of polygamy, in the integration of men and women in worship, in the education of women as part of missionary activity), it is also true that the Catholic Church still clings to a vision of femininity and masculinity, male roles and female roles, man's authority and woman's submission, that makes it a deeply patriarchal institution. This is despite the fact that in the image of Mary as the archetype of the Mother Church and in the feminine identity given to the Church, there is also a powerful matriarchal element in Catholicism. Journeying as we are between the Incarnation and the fulfilment of God's Kingdom on earth, Christians are called to strive to live as a redeemed community that reveals God's love to the world. This cannot happen until Christian patriarchy yields to a loving and egalitarian understanding of human relationships, a restoration to the vision of wholeness in Genesis, when man and woman together make up the image of God.

In speaking of the sin of patriarchy, I do not want to suggest, as some radical feminists do, that women are less sinful than men, or intrinsically better human beings. In societies deeply divided by an unequal distribution of power, those who lack power sometimes practise sins of self-denigration, false humility and a denial of their own worth in the eyes of God. In the parable of the talents, these are the servants who fearfully hide their talents rather than multiplying them, as so many women have done throughout history. (Many others, of course, have struggled desperately to invest their talents wisely, only to have their efforts frustrated and their offering to society rejected.) British and American voting patterns in the last two decades suggest that women are just as willing as men to vote for the politics of greed and self-interest. In a patriarchal society, women sin when they collude in their own oppression as well as when they oppress those lower in the hierarchy of domination than themselves. A matriarchal society would perpetuate other forms of sinfulness, which would necessitate a different kind of critique.

In spite of the advances made by women in some societies in this century, the world today is arguably as patriarchal as it has ever been. The rise in religious fundamentalism is frequently accompanied by a backlash against women's rights, most notably in the American Far Right, in recent pronouncements by the Vatican, and in some Muslim communities. The global eco-

nomic structure, the increasing power of transnational corpora-
tions and the arms trade, have all contributed to an international
climate of competition, aggression and repression. Some writers
use the expression "the feminization of poverty" to refer to the
disproportionate burden that poverty places upon women, as
mothers and frequently as family breadwinners. I think it is also
possible to use this expression to speak of the feminization
of men who, because they are poor, are placed in positions of
powerlessness. Believing as I do that Mary's role as mother of the
poor is essential to an understanding of her, I explore her
significance not only for modern women, but also for the poor in
today's world. Sometimes when I speak of "women" I am
speaking generically. The term "man" has always been used
generically to include woman in the English language. I use the
term "woman" to denote men as well as women who are victims
of or who stand in opposition to the present world order, and who
commit themselves to the creation of a more nurturing and
motherly human community. I also tend to use the word
"womanliness" rather than "femininity," simply because for
many women the latter is a loaded word implying prettiness and
helplessness, while "womanliness" suggests something more substantial and real.

With regard to the language of motherhood, there is a certain
tension implicit in any discussion of the mothering role, because
it is easy to get bogged down in arguments about the extent to
which it is helpful to identify women with motherhood. A
number of writers have made a distinction between the institution of motherhood as a social construct, and the role of mothering as a natural human activity.[2] When I speak about "mothering" I use the word in the latter context. I hope to show not only
why mothering is an essential aspect of being fully human for men
as well as for women, but also why Mary offers a liberative

---

[2] See, for example, Adrienne Rich, *Of Woman Born*. London: Virago (1977)

understanding of the humanity of women that goes far beyond the mothering role. My definition of mothering refers to a way of life and an attitude of mind, and not to the biological function of the female of the species. I do not, however, pretend to be able to resolve the tension that inevitably exists between respecting the biology of motherhood and its physical and emotional claims on women's lives, and the need to liberate women to play a more influential role in the wider community.

Finally on the subject of language, partly for the sake of clarity and because I am writing about Mary as mother and as woman, I have retained the masculine pronoun for God and refer to him as Father, although I believe that ultimately God is both Mother and Father, he and she, just as God is neither Mother nor Father, neither he nor she. However, I also call God Father in juxtaposition to Mary who is Mother. I leave open in this book exactly where Mary stands in relation to the Godhead, but I want to raise the possibility that God is revealed as the Trinitarian Father, Mother and Son in the relationship between God, Mary and Jesus, and that Mary might be the expression of the feminine Spirit of God, breathed into the created world in order to bring the Son into being. I hope to bring out the mutuality and interdependence of Mary's mission and that of Jesus. Neither of them could have fulfilled their calling without the other. My Protestant understanding of Mary was always dictated by the need to keep her firmly rooted in creatureliness lest she usurp her Son. The Catholic Church in recent years has been at pains to distance itself from some of the past excesses of Marian devotion. The Second Vatican Council decided by a narrow margin to incorporate its discussion of Mary into the document on the Church, *Lumen Gentium*, rather than devoting a separate document to her. Although this made Mary more integral to Catholic theology as a whole, it also reinforced the theological distance between Mary and the Godhead that is not always manifest in popular perceptions of Mary. It seems to me that this is an unresolved issue that creates tensions as well as exciting theological possibilities for the future.[3]

This book is intended to stimulate the reader to think about the biblical Mary in a different light. It is not an exhaustive treatment of the subject, but I hope that it will spark new ideas and fresh insights. In bringing my own interpretation to the Gospel accounts of Mary's life, I am indebted to the ideas of others too numerous to mention. I have tried to keep footnotes to a minimum, but I have included in the bibliography those books that have been particularly helpful in shaping my thinking. I am grateful to Liz Crean, Gavin D'Costa, Ursula King and Anne Primavesi for their comments and suggestions during the writing of this book. As a daughter and a mother, my relationship with Mary in all its complexity, joy and struggle is enriched by my relationship with my own mother and my children. My marriage has been a continuous source of love and encouragement, the wellspring from which I draw my energy and my confidence. This book is for Dave and our children, Dylan, Joanna, Daniel and David.

I end this Introduction with an anonymous poem entitled *Mary's Song*:

What have you done to me? What have you made of me?
I cannot find myself in the woman you want me to be ...
Haloed, alone . . . marble and stone: Safe, Gentle, Holy Mary.

My sisters, look at me! Don't turn in pain from me.
Your lives and mine are one in rage and agony ...
Silenced, denied, or sanctified ... Safe, Gentle, Holy Mary.

---

[3] For further discussion of this topic, see Leonardo Boff, *The Maternal Face of God— the Feminine and its Religious Expressions*. London: Collins (1989)

Revolution is my song! MAGNIFICAT proclaims it!
The promise that it makes to us, we dare now to reclaim it!
In our weakness we are strong: wise through pain and grief
　　and wrong ...
Giving, loving, angry women.

All generations will acclaim me only if you can acclaim me ...
Live with joy the truth you find—woman—this is what you
　　name me:
Suffering, proud, prophetic, unbowed ...
Whole, laughing, daughter ... Mary:
Real, warm, living woman ... Mary:
THEN I will be WHOLLY Mary![4]

---

[4] Quoted in Chung Hyun Kyung, *Struggle to be the Sun Again—Introducing Asian Women's Theology*. Maryknoll NY: Orbis Books (1990); London: SCM Press (1989), p. 74

CHAPTER 1

Secret Ecstasy—Mary of Nazareth and the Angel Gabriel

In the sixth month the angel Gabriel was sent by God to a town in Galilee called Nazareth, to a virgin betrothed to a man named Joseph, of the House of David; and the virgin's name was Mary. He went in and said to her, "Rejoice, so highly favoured! The Lord is with you." She was deeply disturbed by these words and asked herself what this greeting could mean, but the angel said to her, "Mary, do not be afraid; you have won God's favour. Listen! You are to conceive and bear a son, and you must name him Jesus. He will be great and will be called Son of the Most High. The Lord God will give him the throne of his ancestor David; he will rule over the House of Jacob for ever and his reign will have no end." Mary said to the angel, "But how can this come about, since I am a virgin?" "The Holy Spirit will come upon you" the angel answered "and the power of the Most High will cover you with its shadow. And so the child will be holy and will be called Son of God. Know this too: your kinswoman Elizabeth has, in her old age, herself conceived a son, and she whom people called barren is now in her sixth month, *for nothing is impossible to God*." "I am the handmaid of the Lord," said Mary "let what you have said be done to me." And the angel left her.

(Luke 1:26-38)

It is easy to imagine Mary as a young woman, soon to be married to Joseph, dreaming of a loving marriage, a family, a home in the village among the people she knew. There, she would lead a quiet life far from the gaze of the Roman occupation, protected from the clamour of the city and the thirst of the desert. She would live in obedience and gentleness, according to the traditions and norms of her people....

But these idyllic domestic images can be ambivalent, and marriage and motherhood never have constituted the sum total of women's dreams. Perhaps Mary experienced the restlessness of spirit common to women who feel torn between the desire for family life and the urge to experience something different. Patriarchal religions are structured in such a way that they deny women the opportunity to be both fully spiritual and fully maternal, because they are concerned primarily with the spiritual needs of the non-maternal male. This sets up a tension in women's lives, a double movement that constitutes the reaching out of the spirit toward eternity and transcendence, and the rootedness of our motherly bodies and emotions in the temporality and turmoil of this life. Mary, too, experienced that double movement. She set out upon the path of conformity and became engaged to Joseph, but she remained open to other possibilities. She was poised before that great Other, the mystery of God setting her apart for a purpose she could not fathom. Although she began to plan her future, she was prepared for radical and unexpected change. Beyond her dreams of normality, there was a more powerful and commanding dream that held her in waiting before the impenetrable silence of the Almighty.

When Mary's dreams were interrupted, when that great silence took form for an instant and became comprehensible, she was afraid but receptive to the angel's message. Her response shows that she knew God had come not to fulfil but to subvert the normal course of events. She was soon to be married and it was quite reasonable that she would conceive and bear Joseph's son, but she challenged the angel: "How can this come about, since I am a virgin?" Mary knew intuitively that the angel's message heralded a watershed event in her life. She had been set apart by God and was being invited to become a unique participant, body, mind and spirit, in the divine will.

The Catholic Church has always insisted on Mary's freedom to choose. She was not a helpless instrument in salvation history. She was free to say no. When in Greek mythology the god Zeus set out to seduce Europa, he embarked on a course of deception in order to win her affection and abduct her. The history of Europe originates in a violent story of divine rape. Christianity originates in a story of mutual loving endeavour between a woman and God. The Annunciation was not an act of seduction but a free invitation to a woman to participate in God's salvific action.

Yet this is not to display an over-anxious concern with ridding the scene of every trace of eroticism. The writings of women mystics such as Teresa of Avila suggest that women's most intense experiences of communion with God are charged with eroticism. Teresa writes of her encounter with a beautiful angel in explicitly erotic imagery:

> In his hands I saw a great golden spear, and at the iron tip there appeared to be a point of fire. This he plunged into my heart several times so that it penetrated to my entrails. When he pulled it out, I felt that he took them with it, and left me utterly consumed by the great love of God. The pain was so severe that it made me utter several moans. The sweetness caused by this intense pain is so extreme that one cannot possibly wish it to cease, nor is one's soul then content with anything but God. This is not a physical, but a spiritual pain, though the body has some share in it—even a considerable share.[1]

---

[1] Teresa of Avila in *The Life of Saint Teresa of Avila by Herself* (tr. J. M. Cohen). London: Penguin Books (1957), p. 210

Elsewhere, referring to her soul as the Bride of God, Teresa speaks of a state of rapture in which

> that soul has now delivered itself into His hands and His great love has so completely subdued it that it neither knows nor desires anything save that God shall do with it what He wills. Never, I think, will God grant this favour save to the soul which He takes for His very own.[2]

Women do not experience sensuality as something compartmentalized and different from other emotional and spiritual experiences. In friendship, prayer and mothering, as well as in sexual relationships, our bodies are receptive and responsive to the impulse of the spirit and the emotions. The French use the word *jouissance* to describe the diffuse sexuality of women's bodies. There is no reason why the erotic language of mysticism should not suggest to us something of the totality of Mary's experience of the Annunciation. But if this encounter was an occasion of profound joy for Mary, it was also one of risk.

While Mary could not possibly have anticipated what lay ahead of her, she knew that it was fraught with danger. The very fact that she agreed to conceive outside marriage meant that she risked death by stoning. She must have considered saying no, choosing instead to remain on the path of relative security that stretched ahead of her, marrying Joseph and enjoying the quietude of a life patterned on generations of wives and mothers. If she said yes, she would embark on a path that was terrifying in its unknowability, shrouded as it was in the whirlwind of God's presence. She could not see where it led and where it would end. To step on to that path would be to break the quiet patterns of life forever, to exchange the familiar for the unknown, the predictable for the

---

[2] Teresa of Avila, "Interior Castle, Fifth Mansion, Chapter II" in David A. Fleming (ed.), *The Fire and the Cloud—An Anthology of Catholic Spirituality.* London: Geoffrey Chapman (1978), p. 238

ever-new and surprising, the concrete realities of life for the word calling her into the whirlwind. It would entail becoming a wayfarer, a person of the wilderness. There was no implicit threat in God's invitation, and no fear of punishment. If she chose the quiet life, she would be left in peace. The decision was hers and hers alone. God waited while Mary deliberated. The history of the world hung in the balance as a young girl considered the options before her. Then she said, "I am the handmaid of the Lord, let what you have said be done to me." And she stepped into the whirlwind.

There is an awesome power in the Annunciation, but the word of God addressed to Mary is also a word of healing and redemption. It is a word of calm—"do not be afraid"—spoken into a disordered and frightening world. But it is also a strange word, an unfamiliar voice breaking into history, and like Mary we are perplexed by the strangeness of the Annunciation. Why do we have Matthew and Luke's accounts of the conception of Jesus? If the story began with his baptism, as in Mark, or with the *Logos* prologue as in John, would it make any difference to our understanding of Jesus' ministry? What does the Virgin Birth tell us about the Kingdom of God? I believe that it is a buried treasure in the Christian heritage, capable of revealing new insights into the nature of salvation and the life of God's Kingdom.

Despite the primal vision of peace and co-operation inherent in most religious traditions, the natural world seems to be governed by laws of violence and competition. Indeed, if our religious traditions were human constructs designed to explain the meaning of life, it is hard to see why most religions are so optimistic. The living world appears to be locked in a battle in which only the fittest survive. This existential chaos pervades the relationship between men and women that is essential to all life and is the basic building block of all communities. Genesis tells us, "In the image of God he created him, male and female he created them" (Gen. 1:27b). In the two creation stories of

23

Genesis we sense the struggle between the primal holistic vision of loving mutuality between the sexes and harmony in the natural world, and the oppressive and arduous realities of life. Confronted with the apparent contradiction between belief in the creative goodness of God and the unjust structuring of the created order, the biblical writers introduce a narrative of sin, fall and redemption into the human story. While the story of Adam and Eve has been used by Christian writers in the past to justify the subordination of women, it is possible to read in it precisely the opposite meaning. The writers of Genesis do not uphold the hierarchical relationship between men and women as a blessing but condemn it as a curse. It is a sign not of the order of creation but of the disorder of a fallen world.

> To the woman he said:
> "I will multiply your pains in childbearing,
> you shall give birth to your children in pain.
> Your yearning shall be for your husband,
> yet he will lord it over you."
>
> (Gen. 3:16)

Woman's pain in childbearing, her yearning for her husband and his domination over her are seen as a deviance from the original relationship between male and female created in the image of God, living as one body naked and without shame in each other's presence. Patriarchy is a consequence of our rebellion against God, and when God makes peace with humankind he breaks the continuity of the patriarchal inheritance by way of the Virgin Birth. Mary's assent to God, her *fiat*, signals the transformative moment in history. In Mary, woman is restored to spiritual wholeness, Eve's long history of blame and misery is ended, and the conflict between the maternal and the spiritual is reconciled. Or that is how it should be, but history tells a different story.

Since the time of the early Church Fathers, Catholic theology has played with images of Eve and Mary without asking what they mean for women. The two have been polarized as whore and virgin, sinner and saint, and women have been roughly divided accordingly. Some women's writings through the centuries reveal a different discourse, a preoccupation with Eve as one who was closer to God in her weakness than Adam was, and one who as precursor to Mary was paradoxically blessed. Christine de Pizan (1365–c.1430), writes:

> And if anyone would say that man was banished because of Lady Eve, I tell you that he gained more through Mary than he lost through Eve when humanity was conjoined to the Godhead, which would never have taken place if Eve's misdeed had not occurred. Thus man and woman should be glad for this sin, through which such an honor has come about. For as low as human nature fell through this creature woman, was human nature lifted higher by this same creature.[3]

Far from seeing Mary and Eve in conflict, such writings suggest female collaboration in the story of salvation. What a contrast there is between this playful, subversive interpretation and the vituperative outburst of Tertullian (160-225), who said of Eve:

> *You* are the Devil's gateway. *You* are the unsealer of that forbidden tree. *You* are the first deserter of the divine Law. *You* are she who persuaded him whom the Devil was not valiant enough to attack. *You* destroyed so easily God's image man. On account of *your* desert, that is death, even the Son of God had to die.[4]

The misogyny that was so completely lacking from Jesus' dealings with women soon began to poison Christian theology. With the language of patriarchy obliterating the early Christian vision of

---

[3] Quoted in Gerda Lerner, *The Creation of Feminist Consciousness—From the Middle Ages to Eighteen-seventy*. New York & Oxford: Oxford University Press (1993), p. 145
[4] Quoted in Rosemary Radford Ruether, *Sexism & God-Talk*. London: SCM Press (1992), p. 167

wholeness, it did not take long before Christianity became a pliable tool in the hands of the imperial patriarchs who have ruled Europe and the Church since the fourth century. But while the Church Fathers have waged their wars on desire and joy and freedom, Mother Church has nurtured and kept alive the fledgling vision of the Gospels that has inspired so many women's struggles through history. In every age there have been women who have rediscovered Eve and Mary's story for themselves, believing their discovery to be unique because their foremothers' voices have been drowned amidst the hubbub of male discourse. In every age there have been women who have reached out across time in solidarity with "Lady Eve," knowing that beneath the label of temptress and whore there is their own humanity struggling to be born, waiting for the one whose *fiat* will one day accomplish what God has promised. In the Virgin Birth, God assures women that he has not forgotten his promise, and that his Word prevails over all the tyranny of history. Man has claimed the right to silence every voice but his, but when God speaks to Mary, he restores the power of speech to woman by explicitly excluding man from the event. Even the task of naming the child, a task sacred to the father, is given to Mary.

I explained in the Introduction that the connection between patriarchy and maleness is a blurred one. Many men are not patriarchal, and many women are. However, patriarchy confers upon men an authority that is denied to women, even if some women manage to break through the barrier and claim some of that authority for themselves, and even if some men choose not to exercise it. In our disordered world men have the power to rule and make decisions, the power of veto, the power to say what will be and what will not be. Western societies may have granted women some small measure of political and social autonomy, but we still live under the curse of Genesis. The yearning for male approval is expressed in the magazines women read, in the cosmetics and fashion industry, in the impossible images of youth and physical perfection that are held up before us, in the eating disorders women suffer from as a consequence of living in a society that teaches them to loathe their own bodies. And while women in affluent societies have been granted some release from the physical terrors and pains of childbirth, we face new and ever more complex psychological and ethical pressures as science lays before us a vast menu of options to control and manipulate our fertility. Childbearing remains a source of pain and damage to many, many women, whether they undergo abortions because their children are not wanted, or subject themselves to intrusive and distressing medical treatment because of the overwhelming pressure to become biological mothers. In many non-Western societies, the lordship of the husband over his wife and the pain of childbearing are as literally true today as they were to the writers of Genesis.

When the angel appears to Mary, we discover that God's will is not under patriarchal control, and Mary herself is liberated from the bondage of the Fall. She is submissive not to Joseph but only to God. The Virgin Birth contradicts Augustine's assertion that

> when she is referred to separately to her quality of "help-meet," which regards the woman herself alone, then she is not the image of God, but as regards the man alone, he is the image of God as fully and completely as when the woman too is joined with him in one.[5]

Thomas Aquinas argued that, although women's subjugation by man was a consequence of the Fall, the subordination of woman to man was part of the hierarchical ordering of creation itself. At the Annunciation, Mary is neither subordinate nor subjugated but stands as an autonomous agent in the presence of God, without any need of a man to make her complete.

---

[5] Quoted in Lerner, *op cit.*, p. 141

But the Annunciation means more than the restoration of woman to spiritual wholeness. It also means the end of the God of patriarchy, the end of the God in whose name wars are waged and the poor are oppressed and human claims to power over one another are lent divine authority. The God of the Annunciation is a God who submits himself to the human will, made manifest in the will of one who has no power and no authority in this world. He is a God who asks to be born of a woman. God sought the permission of a representative of the human race before he came to dwell among us—to do otherwise would have been to override human freedom—but the one appointed to speak on behalf of all people and of all history, the one who represents human freedom before God, was a young Jewish girl, who in her femaleness, her youth and her Jewishness was as far removed from the powers of this world as it is possible to be. She was not even a Jerusalem Jew, but a Nazarene. In John's Gospel, Nathaniel asks when hearing that Jesus is from Nazareth, "Can anything good come from that place?" (John 1:46). In the social hierarchies of her time, Mary was among the lowest of the low. Man, as symbol of the domination of one human being over another, is rendered impotent in the conception of Jesus. To insist on Mary's virginity is to defend the restoration of co-equality to all people in the Kingdom of God. It is to defend the preferential option for the poor, which God exercised in choosing Mary. The new man is born out of the will of God and of a virgin. Only in this way can a world of loving mutuality be restored by a man who was perfect and without sin, including the original sin of the patriarchal inheritance.

The conception of Jesus was a moment of radical discontinuity in the history of humankind, but we can learn as much from what was retained as we can from what was rejected. The power of patriarchy and wealth were destroyed, but all that was good and true in the human condition was given a place in God's earthly Kingdom, including Mary's womanliness and her Jewishness.

While many Old Testament passages depict a patriarchal God, some of the most beautiful metaphors allude to the motherly love of God. God asks Job:

What womb brings forth the ice,
and gives birth to the frost of heaven?
(Job 38:29)

The God of Hosea laments over Israel in the language of a mother, saying, "I was like someone who lifts an infant close against his cheek; stooping down to him I gave him his food" (Hos. 11:4). The Old Testament God hears the distress of barren women like Hannah and Sara (1 Sam. 1 and 2; Gen. 21), he is a God who blesses the love between Ruth and her mother-in-law, Naomi, he is a God who intervenes on Susanna's behalf when she is falsely accused of adultery (Dan. 13).

In recent years, and after a shameful history of blame and divisiveness, the Catholic Church has at last recognized the authenticity of the Jewish religion, calling the Jews our "older brothers in faith." Perhaps more importantly, though, the Jewish religion is the older sister of Christianity, sharing the same vision of the motherly Kingdom of God that will come to be in the Bride and the Mother, in Zion and Jerusalem.

Rejoice, Jerusalem,
be glad for her, all you who love her!
Rejoice, rejoice for her,
all you who mourned her!

That you may be suckled, filled,
from her consoling breast,
that you may savour with delight
her glorious breasts.
(Isa. 66:10-11)

29

If we speak of discontinuity in the event of the Incarnation, we must also speak of continuity. If we see in the conception of Christ a divine challenge to the law of patriarchy, we must also see a divine affirmation of the power of motherly love that permeates the Hebrew Scriptures and the Christian Bible. In Christ, the power of the patriarchal law is broken and the motherly Kingdom is announced. Mary, the Mother of God and the archetype of the Church, is also the daughter of Zion. She is both ancient and modern, both old and new, containing within her own body the promised reconciliation of all the rivalries and divisions of history.

By meditating on the circumstances of the Annunciation, we can glimpse the shape of the Kingdom of God that is both here and still to come, and we can learn to recognize both Christianity's past failures and its future mission. The history of the Church sometimes seems to be the very opposite of God's Kingdom on earth. Yet the fact that we recognize what we are in the process of becoming, the willingness of the Church to affirm for two thousand years, in spite of its own failings, that on a quiet night in Nazareth, a Jewish girl and the God of all creation met and a new world was born, gives us hope. It is a sign of the Kingdom within us, a Kingdom that for all our many failures still spills over into the world and proclaims itself to all humankind.

Like Mary, we may initially be afraid of the implications of saying yes to God's Kingdom on earth. To break free of the old rules that both restrain and reassure us is difficult. If we live in the Western democracies, our acquiescence in global structures of oppression is bought with material benefits and improvements in lifestyle that are hard to surrender. Christians in the West need urgently to be reminded that the Kingdom of God is a political Kingdom—it is not a Kingdom of individualism but a Kingdom of community.

In the domestic world as well, the old hierarchies have a certain reassuring familiarity about them. Men have not only ruled women, they have also protected and provided for them. Kept in a state of more or less comfortable dependence, it is easy for women to cling to security and to shy away from the kind of choices that faced Mary. We are trained to believe that the fulfilment of womanhood lies in obedience, in upholding social norms, in treading the familiar paths of life and doing what is expected of us. Women value reliability more than daring, and we are wary of what is exhilarating and challenging. But valuing the precious world of the family as we do, reassured by its promise of security and continuity, seduced by traditional role models, we nevertheless glimpse other ways of being. We are not made for repetition and conformity. The voice of God calls us out of old patterns of living, and invites us to step into the unknown. Like Mary, we may be deeply disturbed by the choices we are asked to make. She shows us that we come to the fullness of our being by choosing the unknown path, the road into newness. Sometimes we must have the courage not to do what is expected of us. We must be willing to break the rules and flaunt the conventions of society, to refuse to collude in systems of oppression and injustice, not in order to conform to the dreary cult of individualism, but in order to forge new paths that others might follow.

For centuries Mary has been held up to women as an idol, for it is idolatrous to suggest that self-abnegation and subservience are the way to godliness. Only false gods are worshipped by bondage and fear. When we discover the biblical Mary stripped free of patriarchal interpretation, we discover a different model for the Christian life. She is a free spirit, an adventurer. She calls her sisters forward along a rocky path, and she teaches us that discipleship is a constant breaking free, a passionate openness to the God of life. The traditional hymn speaks of Mary as "that mother mild." When my daughter was three years old, she came to me one day and said, "Why was Mary wild?" "I don't think Mary was wild," I replied. "Yes she was," she said. "Don't you know that song we sing about her—'Mary was that mother wild, Jesus Christ her little child'?" In a sense, Mary was wild, gloriously and liberatingly wild. That is why we cannot follow her in straight lines, in docile lives patterned too simplistically either on virginity or on motherhood. We must become daughters of the spirit and the truth, women of the wind that blows where it will, seekers who follow our star through the wilderness. We must learn to dance as Mary did to the music of God, barefoot and daring, weaving our stories into the "wild web" of Mary's faith. Like Gerard Manley Hopkins in his poem, *The Blessed Virgin Compared to the Air We Breathe*, we must learn to recognize the pervasive wonder of Mary's faith that is as necessary to us as the air we breathe.

"Rejoice, so highly favoured! The Lord is with you." How many of us know how to rejoice in our faith? Mary has been a symbol of women's subordination for too long. Let us make her instead a symbol of women's courage and rejoicing in the presence of the Lord.

The following poem, called *Be it Unto Me*, suggests something of the wild grandeur of the Annunciation:

Let in the wind
Let in the rain
Let in the moors tonight.

The storm beats on my window-pane,
Night stands at my bed-foot,
Let in the fear,
Let in the pain,
Let in the trees that toss and groan,
Let in the north tonight.

Let in the nameless formless power
That beats on my door,
Let in the ice, let in the snow,
The banshee howling on the moor,
The bracken-bush on the bleak hillside,
Let in the lost tonight ...

Fearful is my virgin heart
And frail my virgin form,
And must I then take pity on
The raging of the storm
That rose up from the great abyss
Before the earth was made,
That pours the stars in cataracts
And shakes this violent world?
Let in the fire,
Let in the power,
Let in the invading might.

Gentle must my fingers be
And pitiful my heart
Since I must bind in human form
A living power so great,
A living impulse wild and great
That cries about my house
With all the violence of desire
Desiring this, my peace.

Pitiful my heart must hold
The lonely stars at rest,
Have pity on the raven's cry
The torrent and the eagle's wing
The icy waters of the tarn
 And on the biting blast.

Let in the wound,
Let in the pain,
Let in your child tonight.

                                        (Anon.)

CHAPTER 2

Envisioning a New World—
Mary Visits Elizabeth

Mary set out at that time and went as quickly as she could to a town in the hill country of Judah. She went into Zechariah's house and greeted Elizabeth. Now as soon as Elizabeth heard Mary's greeting, the child leapt in her womb and Elizabeth was filled with the Holy Spirit. She gave a loud cry and said, "Of all women you are the most blessed, and blessed is the fruit of your womb. Why should I be honoured with a visit from the mother of my Lord? For the moment your greeting reached my ears, the child in my womb leapt for joy. Yes, blessed is she who believed that the promise made her by the Lord would be fulfilled."

And Mary said:

"My soul proclaims the greatness of the Lord
and my spirit exults in God my saviour;
because he has looked upon his lowly handmaid.
Yes, from this day forward all generations will call me blessed,
for the Almighty has done great things for me.
Holy is his name,
and his mercy reaches from age to age for those who fear him.
He has shown the power of his arm,
He has routed the proud of heart.

He has pulled down princes from their thrones and exalted the
lowly.
The hungry he has filled with good things, the rich sent empty
away.
He has come to the help of Israel his servant, mindful of his mercy
—according to the promise he made to our ancestors—
of his mercy to Abraham and to his descendants for ever."

Mary stayed with Elizabeth about three months and then went back
home.

(Luke 1:39-56)

When Mary sings the *Magnificat,* she evokes the words of
Hannah, the mother of Samuel, so that as we read this passage in
Luke we are in the company of three women. Hannah's story is
told in 1 Samuel. She was one of Elkanah's two wives. His other
wife, Penninah, had children but Hannah had none, and for this
reason Elkanah gave Penninah preferential treatment, even
though he loved Hannah more. Elkanah had some trouble
understanding Hannah's longing for children, because he thought
he ought to be more than enough for any woman. Eli, the priest,
seeing how fervently Hannah prayed in the temple, accused her
of being drunk. Eventually, Hannah struck a bitter deal. If God
would give her a son, she would dedicate him to God. Hannah's
hymn in the temple at the dedication of her child, Samuel,
inspired the *Magnificat.* Rewarding her faithfulness, God blessed
Hannah with several more children.

I want to spend some time considering Hannah, because her
unseen presence in the words of the *Magnificat* invites compari-
son. Why did Mary evoke Hannah in her great hymn of
thanksgiving?

Hannah's life manifests the suffering of women, not in the
sense of Mary's purposeful and visionary suffering, but in the
sense of the suffering described in Genesis—the suffering of
women as victims in a world where mutuality has given way to

dominance and servility. African women speak of the discord and jealousy inherent in polygamous relationships, of the rivalry between wives and the bitterness of infertility in societies that value women primarily as childbearers. Hannah inhabits a world of discord between men and women, and between one woman and another. Eli the priest initially interprets her fervent prayer as drunkenness. (Religious women throughout the ages have found their spirituality misinterpreted and condemned by male priests!) Perhaps Mary, bearing the brunt of the gossip in Nazareth, castigated by the priests for being pregnant outside marriage, identified with Hannah's lonely struggle.

Hannah's world is still our world today. Very little has changed. It must be said again and again that the Kingdom of God has come and is still to come. The *Magnificat* rejoices in God's Kingdom made present to Mary in the dazzling light of her encounter with God, but for us that Kingdom remains the first pale light on the horizon of time. The darkness is less dense than it was, we begin to discern shapes and colours, we have some inkling of what the world might look like when daylight comes, but there are long shadows and dark corners, and our eyes deceive us in the gloom. When we look for ways to interpret Hannah's story, we are using the past in order to map out future territory. We are beginning to get a feel for the world that we have come from and the world that we are moving toward, a world that we are also called to build along the way.

The Old Testament is a book of the desert, written by people for whom barrenness and fertility were powerful contrasting symbols of the environment they lived in. A number of the women of the Bible were barren women made fertile by God, such as Sara, Hannah and Elizabeth. For a people who were small in number, outnumbered by their enemies, living in the physical landscape of the wilderness, fecundity was a sign of God's blessing. The fertile woman, like the fertile land, signalled God's loving care for his people and his pledge for the future.

In Hannah's song and in the *Magnificat*, however, God's presence is manifest not in the physical function of childbearing, but in the creation of a world of justice and the ending of tyranny. Hannah and Mary did not see mothering in terms of a biological function and a private domestic role. As mothers they reinterpreted the world, seeing in their own experience an affront to the arrogant and the powerful and a vindication of the oppressed, those whom Hannah symbolized by "the barren woman" in her song. God's Kingdom is a motherly Kingdom, most perfectly glimpsed through the eyes of two women who in becoming mothers recognized the essence of that Kingdom.

The communities that we create on earth must be measured against the yardstick of the biblical Kingdom. A good community is one that mothers its people, teaching them to live together in harmony, nurturing the young and protecting the weak and the old. Mothering is the concrete expression of hope and love in human relationships, bringing gentleness and wisdom to our struggle for survival, making us concerned for those who are vulnerable, teaching us to work in co-operation with one another and the natural world for the good of all creation. If we understand stewardship in terms of mothering the world rather than governing it, we will understand the role God assigned to Adam and Eve. Throughout Christian history, there have been women who have continued to affirm the motherly love of God in the face of the growing power of patriarchal language. Julian of Norwich spoke of God as mother, and Hildegard of Bingen described all the divine attributes of love, justice and wisdom as feminine. "Divine love was in eternity, and, in the beginning of all sanctity, she brought forth all creatures without any mixture of evil, and she brought forth Adam and Eve from the immaculate earth."[1] The following poem was pinned on a woman's bedroom

---

[1] Hildegard writing to Abbot Adam in *The Letters of Hildegard of Bingen* Vol. I (tr. Joseph L. Baird and Radd K. Ehrman), New York, London: Oxford University Press (1994), p. 194

wall in Mexico. A friend doing research visited this woman, whose name is Antonia, and said that "her living conditions were the most basic I came across."

> To be a mother
> is a sweet sorrow
> It is to give
> because we choose to give.
> It is to be
> twice over.
> It is to beat
> like a double heart,
> to see
> without having to look,
> to love
> before getting to know,
> to believe
> in life beyond,
> to feel
> the presence of God.

These are the values that would shine out of any community made in the image of the Kingdom of God—the sweet sorrow of mothering, the risk of love that stakes everything on the unknown other, and the abundance of life lived twice over, in the presence of God and in the sunrise of eternity.

If this is what mothering symbolizes, then we should ask what barrenness symbolizes. Hannah knew from her own experience what it was to be regarded as worthless in the eyes of society. The barren woman is the person who is no longer valued as a productive member of the community. She is barren because she longs to give of herself, to give of her life and her love and her vitality, but nobody wants what she has to offer. Advanced capitalism is an extreme form of patriarchy that makes us all barren women, trapped in impersonal social structures that deny our need to live in mutual dependence and solicitude. In all the millions of words that clutter our public lives, we are less and less able to find a way to speak of compassion, faith and love, because the markets will only allow us a common language of greed and self-interest. If the motherly community is one in which each person is known by name, treasured for her unique gifts and abilities, nurtured in her weakness and encouraged in her strength, then the barren society is one in which people become numbers, the mass media become a substitute for creative individuality, and the moral weakness of the rich is used as a tool of oppression in the war against the powerless.

Elizabeth was the last barren woman mentioned in the Bible to experience God's presence in the physical manifestation of pregnancy. Elizabeth's child would announce that the Kingdom of God was at hand, and in that Kingdom, with their personhood restored, women would become co-workers on an equal footing with men, valued not just in terms of their childbearing potential but as people of faith and vision. Of the women who came to Jesus for healing, we are not told of any who were barren. We know nothing of the maternal status of his women followers such as Martha and Mary and Mary Magdalene. Jesus loves women not as bearers of children but as people of worth and dignity in their own right. Nowhere does the New Testament suggest that women should see their role primarily in terms of motherhood. Christ invites us all, men and women, to become human beings who nurture one another and who give new life to the destitute, the hopeless, to those who are small and unprotected in this brutal world. This is the only kind of fertility that is of enduring value in the Kingdom of God.

However, in rejecting the belief so precious to popes and churchmen that women are fulfilled primarily in motherhood, it is important not to trivialize the impact of motherhood on women's lives. In God's Kingdom, women and men will be fully restored to the wholeness of being male and female created in the image of God. We share in the work of that restoration by striving to create conditions of equality and justice in this world, but in our striving we are still embodied human beings, and for women this means we continue to experience our fertile bodies as sources of both delight and grief. The desire for children conflicts with our desire to play a role in the public domain, because modern society is so structured to make it very difficult for women to do both without considerable stress. While most of us feel a strong need to express ourselves in motherhood, we also long to have what men have conferred upon them as a birthright—the power to mould and shape society, the right to speak for and about ourselves, the freedom to describe the world as we see it and to have that perspective incorporated fully into the policies and philosophies and principles of those who order the priorities of our lives.

Pregnancy is an ambivalent experience for women, signifying both gain and loss, both the joy of birth and the fear of death. Society also has an ambivalent attitude toward pregnancy, on the one hand treating it with a sense of awe and wonder, and on the other hand surrounding pregnant women with taboos and superstitions. During the debate about the ordination of women in the Church of England, a number of men and women admitted to feeling uncomfortable about the prospect of a pregnant woman administering the sacraments. When the film star Demi Moore appeared heavily pregnant and naked on a magazine cover, people were scandalized. The symbolic power of the pregnant woman is resented in patriarchal society. She symbolizes the limits of man's control. Her body represents something fearful and mysterious to the man who, having performed the brief function of impregnation, is no longer essential to the process of procreation. The taboos that surround her are designed to disempower her. The cycles of women's fertility are an unwelcome reminder to those who desire to master the earth that our human biology is mysteriously and powerfully attuned to the natural world. It is no coincidence that the scientific manipulation of women's fertility increases in direct proportion to the scientific manipulation of the earth's fertility. Both are expressive of the patriarchal desire to subjugate the natural world and to harness the cycles of life to the agenda of profit and power. Man will not have fully mastered nature until he has mastered the pregnant woman, and it is a worrying feature of modern life that despite twenty-five years of feminism, Western man is very close to achieving both these objectives.

But pregnancy retains its mysterious power, and even in our technological age the newness of life generates a sense of awe and wonder. Pregnant women are the embodiment of the future, and the community depends on them for its survival. They symbolize hope, fertility and creative power. They make visible God's commitment to the continued creation of the human being in his and her own image. Like the rainbow, they are a sign of God's promise. In an age when legitimate concerns about over-population veer perilously close to becoming an anti-life ideology, we must preserve our sense of wonder at the miracle of new life made visible in the pregnant woman.

In Mary's visit to Elizabeth, we see that pregnant women, treated with such ambivalence in the world of men, are chosen by God as the special bearers of his word. Hannah, the barren wife, was fertile and creative in the eyes of God. He gave her a new song to sing, a prophecy that would endure until her distant sister Mary took up her song and fulfilled it. God struck dumb the male priest Zechariah and restored the power of speech to pregnant women. The barren Hannah, the elderly Elizabeth and the virgin Mary stand before us, round-bellied and joyful, affirming the restoration of all women in every stage and condition of life to their rightful place in the human community.

The Visitation is often portrayed in a way that reinforces a certain dreary image of women as submissive and dutiful caregivers, with the young Mary ignoring her own discomfort to go and help her older cousin. I imagine Mary setting out with wings on her heels to seek the companionship of the one person in all the world who would understand the uniqueness of her situation, and who would share in the delight of her pregnancy. In going to stay with Elizabeth, she found refuge away from the gossiping women of Nazareth in the presence of a woman who was in every sense her soulmate. In Mary and Elizabeth we see the power of a friendship that was not a duty or a burden but a joyful expression of mutually affirming love.

The disciples of Jesus were often locked in competition with one another for first place. There was no such rivalry between Mary and Elizabeth. Elizabeth recognized immediately the primacy of Mary's calling, and her greeting to Mary was a radiant expression of generosity toward the younger woman. John the Baptist would inherit his mother's humility, saying of Jesus, "I am not fit to kneel down and undo the strap of his sandals" (Mark 1:7). God condemns hierarchies based on power, race and gender, but without some ranking of vocations and responsibilities society would collapse. Through Elizabeth and John, we learn how to be gracious in second place, how to respond to greatness in others.

Mary and Elizabeth's relationship is in direct contrast to that of Hannah and Peninnah. In Hannah and Peninnah, we see the bitterness and the hurt, the jealousy and resentment that breed in an unjust environment. People need to feel valued and loved to be able to give of themselves freely to others. Mary and Elizabeth, in the perfect assurance of God's love for them, experienced a transformed and transforming friendship. In them, we see what women mean to one another in the redeemed community. Between them, these two had been given the power to change the world.

What can we learn from Mary's great hymn of praise sung in the presence of Elizabeth? Unlike Hannah and Elizabeth, Mary had not been praying for a child. Her pregnancy was not God's answer to her request—rather, it was her answer to God's request. It represented a crisis, creating problems in her relationship with Joseph and jeopardizing her standing in the community. It changed the direction of her life, and began a process of self-discovery and growing awareness of the mystery and power of God's love. For Elizabeth, pregnancy was an unadulterated blessing and joy, a clear answer to prayer. For Mary it was surely a more complex experience. The journey from Nazareth to Judah would have left her feeling tired and vulnerable. Perhaps she had left unresolved business behind her. Did she go away to give Joseph time to think about what to do? Did she find the atmosphere in the town intolerable as news of her pregnancy spread? In the warmth of Elizabeth's presence, Mary was at last free to express the intensity of her emotions and her dreams. I picture her running the last few yards to Elizabeth's front door, breathless and laughing and crying with relief, sweeping her elderly cousin into her arms and dancing with exhilaration as at last she found a space in which to express herself.

The *Magnificat* is astonishing in its scope. It is the realization of Mary's role as Mother of God and mother of the poor. It is a hymn that soars up to heaven and extends to the ends of the earth. In the intimate experience of pregnancy, Mary weaves together body and soul, heaven and earth, and she celebrates the connection between herself and all of creation. There is much talk today of interconnectedness and holism. It has been said that the flutter of a butterfly's wing creates a ripple in the cosmos. In the *Magnificat*, a young Jewish girl praises God, and her small voice ripples out to the far corners of the universe and to the beginning and end of time.

But the *Magnificat* is also a song of courage. Even as these two pregnant women hugged each other and laughed and danced with joy, they knew something of the forces they were up against. In teaching their sons to become children of the *Magnificat*, they would teach them to be dangerous subversives. Mary and

Elizabeth were wild women whose wild sons would be killed by those who could not bear the wild beauty of the human spirit. The *Magnificat* is more than an eschatological vision of the Kingdom of God. Its language is revolutionary, its dream of liberation formed by the day-to-day experience of living in an occupied state under an oppressive regime. Many people in Latin America, Asia and Africa find it an inspiring manifesto for resistance and change. In the Lord's prayer, we pray for God's Kingdom to come on earth. The *Magnificat* tells us what that Kingdom is like. It is a Kingdom in which preference is given to those who derive no benefit from the economic and political structures of power in this world. It is a motherly Kingdom, prophesied by a pregnant woman, crushed underfoot by the powers of this world, but rising again and again on the lips of women who know that in the affirmation of Mary's full humanity, the whole human race is affirmed. "Blessed is she who believed that the promise made her by the Lord would be fulfilled." Blessed are we, when we too dare to believe.

CHAPTER 3

The Journey Toward Birth—
Mary and Joseph on the Road
to Bethlehem

Now at this time Caesar Augustus issued a decree for a census of the whole world to be taken. This census—the first—took place while Quirinius was governor of Syria, and everyone went to his own town to be registered. So Joseph set out from the town of Nazareth in Galilee and travelled up to Judaea, to the town of David called Bethlehem, since he was of David's House and line, in order to be registered together with Mary, his betrothed, who was with child.
(Luke 2:1-5)

In the *Magnificat*, Mary set her face toward God's Kingdom and against the powers of this world. Now the powers of this world set their face against Mary and her unborn child, and this is a process that will be repeated again and again in her life. This great struggle between good and evil, between love and tyranny, is played out on a vast stage and the actions of the powerful are often protected by anonymity and impersonality. The language and processes of oppression are dehumanized to such an extent that there may be very little connection between the bureaucrat doing his job and families evicted from their homes, forced into hardship, deprived of a living, and at the far end of bureaucratic efficiency, imprisoned and tortured for having the wrong ideas or murdered for being the wrong race.

Nobody set out to "get" Mary. There was no malicious schemer who rubbed his hands together and asked how he could make Jesus' birth as difficult as possible. Those who enforced the census and made pregnant women travel long distances without security or provision for the birth of their children may have felt genuine regret and pity, but what could they do? After all, they were only doing their job. There was a census to be taken, the needs of the State to be met.

When we allow the structures of bureaucracy to take precedence over all else, we invert the godly order of our world. We break the first commandment—"I am the Lord your God. You shall have no other gods before me"—when we put human beings in the service of institutions. We have been created to serve God alone, the God of all love and compassion and peace. We are not created to serve the idols of technology and market forces. Every time somebody obediently bows down before these idols made by human hands, somebody somewhere suffers. A person too poor and impotent to work the system becomes its victim.

The Gospel of prosperity is a dangerous heresy in the Christian church today, spreading as it does the belief that God rewards faith with wealth, that if we are struggling or poor, it must be because we are not praying hard enough or there is some unconfessed sin in our lives for which we are being punished. This not only sanctifies the excessive wealth of some First World Christians, it also becomes a way of bribing Christians in poorer countries to conform to the capitalist agenda and blunts the radical message of the Gospel. Even if we consider ourselves immune to such ideas, I think most of us strike bargains with God at some time in our lives, or succumb to the temptation to see problems as signs of divine displeasure. It is easy to believe that if we are doing what God wants us to do, things should go smoothly. If we encounter obstacles, particularly if we have embarked on a project that has entailed making a difficult choice, our confidence is quickly eroded by doubt and anxiety. A friend whose husband fell ill soon after she started a fulfilling career wondered aloud if this was God's sign to her that she should not be working. She should be at home looking after the family. If God had wanted her to work, surely he would have made it easier for her?

Mary's experience teaches us that the purpose of God is more mysterious than that, and to follow him requires a faith that does not demand worldly approval or visible signs of affirmation. We follow God in darkness, knowing that God himself is the meaning and the end of our journey. Along the way, there will inevitably be times of peace and tranquillity and times of struggle and hardship. Sometimes both our happiness and our problems may be attributable to our own actions, but for much of the time explanations do not come so easily. Life's joys and heartaches cannot be seen in simplistic terms of reward and punishment. Mary had found favour with God. She was blessed among women and full of grace. The child she was carrying was the Son of God. Surely, she was entitled to a quiet confinement and a gentle birth? Instead, her faith was stretched to the utmost in the situation in which she found herself. The journey to Bethlehem witnesses to the tenacity of Mary's faith. Had she been less assured in her inner life that she was doing the will of God, perhaps she would have misread the signs, begun to doubt her experience of the Annunciation, interpreted her troubles as a sign of divine displeasure. Her example strengthens us when we find our dreams and visions trapped in the quagmire of bureaucracy and political obstructions, or when we do what we believe is right only to find ourselves in greater trouble than when we started. So often in our journey toward our encounter with Christ, we set out in what feels like a radiant glow of inspiration, only to discover our plans thwarted and our energies depleted. In Mary, we learn to recognize this as part of the journey, and to have faith that at the end we will indeed encounter a star and experience a birthing.

Joseph struggled alongside Mary on the journey to Bethlehem, sharing her helplessness in the face of the occupying force of Rome. If Mary represents the autonomy of woman before God in the event of Jesus' conception, what does Joseph represent? God asked Joseph to agree to something that is supremely difficult for men shaped by the values of patriarchy. He asked Joseph to marry a woman who was pregnant with someone else's child. In the last chapter I discussed the symbolic power of pregnancy, but to the patriarchal fear of the power of nature we should perhaps add the even deeper fear engendered by questions about paternity. A woman knows the children she bears are her own, but for a man there can be no such absolute certainty. Joseph loved Mary enough to bend the rules of patriarchy. When he learned of her pregnancy, his first instinct was to protect her from scandal by ending their betrothal privately (Matt. 1:19), even although he had a public duty to expose Mary's supposed adultery. However, God asked Joseph to go even further, to break the rules altogether and to assume responsibility for Mary's child. There is a poignant Gaelic poem called *The First Miracle of Christ* that contemplates Joseph's distress. It also portrays Mary as deeply sensuous. Mary and Joseph are walking in a wood where fruit trees grow, and in a reversal of the story of Adam and Eve, Mary asks Joseph to give her the fruit to eat.

That was the time when she was great,
That she was carrying the King of grace,
And she took a desire for the fruit
That was growing on the gracious slope.

Then spoke Mary to Joseph,
in a voice low and sweet:
"Give to me of the fruit, Joseph,
That I may quench my desire."

And Joseph spoke to Mary,
And the hard pain in his breast:
"I will give thee of the fruit, Mary,
But who is the father of thy burthen?"

Then it was that the Babe spoke,
From out of her womb:
"Bend ye down every beautiful bough,
That my Mother may quench her desire."

And from the bough that was highest,
To the bough that was lowest,
They all bent down to her knee,
And Mary partook of the fruit
In her loved land of prophecy.

Then Joseph said to Mary,
And he full of heavy contrition,
"It is carrying Him thou art,
The King of glory and of grace.
Blessed art thou, Mary,
    Among the women of all lands.
Blessed art thou, Mary,
    Among the women of all lands."[1]

On the road to Bethlehem, having accepted Mary and her baby
and having braved the gossip that surrounded her pregnancy,
Joseph found himself stripped of his traditional role as provider
and protector. The *Protevangelium* of James, part of the apocry-
phal literature of the second century, includes a moving account
of Joseph's concern for Mary, but also of his perplexity and his
lack of confidence.

---

[1] See Alexander Carmichael, *Carmina Gadelica - Hymns and Incantations*. Trowbridge:
Floris Books (1992), pp 171-2

Now there went out a decree from the king Augustus that all inhabitants of Bethlehem in Judaea should be enrolled. And Joseph said: "I shall enrol my sons, but what shall I do with this child? How shall I enrol her? As my wife? I am ashamed to do that. Or as my daughter? But all the children of Israel know that she is not my daughter. . . . And they came half the way, and Mary said to him: "Joseph, take me down from the ass, for the child within me presses me, to come forth." And he took her down there and said to her: "Where shall I take you and hide your shame? For the place is desert."[2]

At the end of Mary's pregnancy, Joseph was unable to meet her basic physical needs for rest and a comfortable birthing place. His masculinity symbolized nothing. He struggled alongside his wife and shared her impotence. Deprived of their social roles, their sense of belonging and all outward signs of status and identity, the couple on the road to Bethlehem represent the little people of this world, the people who are forever migrants and refugees because they are small cogs in the vast impersonal machines of power. Their needs pale into insignificance beside the demands of the State. It would have mattered nothing to the powers that be if this pregnant woman had died in childbirth. The lives of the poor are cheap.

But stripped of all comfort and protection, Mary was not alone. Again and again in these reflections on the biblical Mary, we will encounter her friends and travelling companions. God was with Mary in Joseph's companionship on the road to Bethlehem. When we look for God's presence in our lives, we must look not for signs but for people. God's love rarely comes to us as an abstract mystical force. It is almost always incarnate, channelled through human agents, expressed and experienced only in community. Perhaps that is why at those moments when we find

2 "The Protevangelium of James" in E. Hennecke, *New Testament Apocrypha*. London: Lutterworth Press (1963), p. 383

ourselves absolutely alone in the core of our existence, at the moment of birth and death or in the depths of terror and pain, we experience God as Absence, as the One who forsakes us. As long as there is some conscious part of our being that can reach out to another, as long as we are aware of another person's concern, we sense the presence of God. *Ubi caritas et amor, Deus ibi est.* Mary and Joseph made God present to one another on the road to Bethlehem, and together they prayed for the child who was coming to birth, the child who would make God present to all humankind.

CHAPTER 4

A Manger and a Murmur of Angels—Mary Gives Birth to Jesus

While they were there the time came for her to have her child, and she gave birth to a son, her first-born. She wrapped him in swaddling clothes, and laid him in a manger because there was no room for them at the inn. In the countryside close by there were shepherds who lived in the fields and took it in turns to watch their flocks during the night. The angel of the Lord appeared to them and the glory of the Lord shone round them. They were terrified, but the angel said, "Do not be afraid. Listen, I bring you news of a great joy, a joy to be shared by the whole people. Today in the town of David a saviour has been born to you: he is Christ the Lord. And here is a sign for you: you will find a baby wrapped in swaddling clothes and lying in a manger." And suddenly with the angel there was a great throng of the heavenly host, praising God and singing:

"Glory to God in the highest heaven,
and peace to men who enjoy his favour."

Now when the angels had gone from them into heaven, the shepherds said to one another, "Let us go to Bethlehem and see this thing that has happened which the Lord has made known to us." So they hurried away and found Mary and Joseph, and the baby lying in the manger. When they saw the child they repeated what they had been told about him, and everyone who heard it was astonished at what the shepherds had to say. As for Mary, she treasured all these things and pondered them in her heart.

(Luke 2:6-19)

After Jesus had been born at Bethlehem in Judaea during the reign of King Herod, some wise men came to Jerusalem from the east. "Where is the infant king of the Jews?" they asked. "We saw his star as it rose and have come to do him homage." ... Having listened to what the king had to say, they set out. And there in front of them was the star they had seen rising; it went forward and halted over the place where the child was. The sight of the star filled them with delight, and going into the house they saw the child with his mother Mary, and falling to their knees they did him homage.

(Matt. 2:1-2, 9-11)

"She gave birth to a son." In the Introduction, I spoke about reading meaning into silence. The word "birth" opens into a world of meaning. The woman in childbirth is on the threshold of life and death. Her body struggles to bring the future into being, but her pain and exhaustion consume her to the point where she experiences a dying as well as a birthing, a loss of self, of identity and control and dignity, a loss of all the protective layers with which we surround ourselves. When a woman gives birth to her firstborn child, she too is born. She is born as a mother, born into a new identity and a new world of relationship and commitment that surpasses anything she has known before. To say this is not to idealize motherhood. I have worked on research in which mothers who had surrendered their children for adoption were interviewed, as were mothers whose children had been taken into care because of neglect or abuse. In every case, the mother remained bound to the life of her child by a powerful love that the severing of the physical bond between them could not break. A woman cannot give birth without dying and rising again, and sometimes both the dying and the rising are painful beyond endurance. Birth and death are very close to one another, marking the completion of the life cycle, the point of entry into and departure from the human world, our birthing into life and our birthing into death and beyond. When Jesus died on the cross, his physical passion was Mary's spiritual passion—it was the sword piercing her soul (Luke 2:35). In Jesus' birth, Mary underwent her own physical passion. Rejected by society and lying in a barn among animals, she suffered for the salvation of the world.

It has been argued that Mary, free from original sin, would not have suffered in childbirth because such suffering is a consequence of the Fall and of the curse visited upon Eve. This is a form of docetism, manifesting the same kind of refusal to come to terms with our bodily realities that led the docetists to argue that Jesus only appeared to suffer and die on the cross. Jesus' birth was as real as his death. Mary gave birth as all women do, with her womb contracting and her muscles stretching and her flesh tearing to bring her baby into the world. Water and blood poured from her body in the birthing process. God entered the world through a woman's vagina.

Catholic writers and artists have always shown a reluctance to portray the physical realities of Jesus' birth. While some have described in literal and graphic detail the agony of the crucifixion, the birth of Jesus seems to be trapped in a timeless sentimental image of the stable and the shepherds with a Madonna who appears free from all traces of childbirth. I wonder if anyone has ever painted a blood-stained Madonna with the grimace and sweat of birth on her face. I suspect most women who have experienced childbirth find themselves alienated from rather than identifying with Mary's experience as perceived by celibate men, whose preoccupation with the state of Mary's hymen sometimes descends into a distasteful kind of theological prurience. To suggest that Mary's ruptured hymen would put an end to her capacity to serve God in perfect love is to reject the natural processes of women's bodies, created and ordained by God. It is also to take an astonishingly mechanistic view of both birth and sexuality, implying that what matters more than anything else is not the nature of the act (in this case two completely different acts), but the physical tearing of a piece of skin.

Yet the Catholic imagination that shies away from the womanly realities of birth is only part of the story. As always in Catholicism, there are womanly images just beneath the surface, and I believe that many women through the ages have been able to tap into this subterranean life of the Church and find comfort and meaning in it, because it conforms to what women themselves experience of life. My third child was born on Boxing Day, and I found myself preoccupied during the later stages of pregnancy with thoughts of Mary. However, in the Presbyterian Church to which I belonged, we did not celebrate Advent and there was no sense of expectation and waiting for the birth of Christ. How could there be, in those branches of Christianity that have expunged the power of Mary from their worship? It was only after becoming a Catholic that I discovered the rich meaning of Advent, the sense of the Mother Church and indeed of the whole world being caught up in a state of expectation as we await the coming of Christ. In the Advent readings and liturgies there is a great depth of reflection and repentance, of grappling with the meaning and the purpose of our lives. In Advent, pregnancy becomes a spiritual condition that we all share, women and men alike, and the raw power of the pregnant woman is communicated throughout the Church, belying the anodyne plaster Madonnas who beam down on us.

It is also true that although the Church prepares with great solemnity for the birth of Christ, I suspect most of us experience Advent and Christmas as something of a spiritual anti-climax. We resolve to prepare ourselves, to be at peace with God and the world, to move toward Christmas in a spirit of quiet contemplation, and we find ourselves instead frantically shopping and cooking and rushing around, so that the spirituality of Christmas is crowded out by the pressures of the secular world. But for Mary too, the first Christmas was not what she expected. It was an anti-climax for her too. She did not spend her time quietly preparing for the birth of her child, and when he was born she found herself alone and forsaken by God and by her fellow human beings as she sweated and bled on her bed of straw. Perhaps she remembered the Annunciation, that rare mystical moment when God was fully present to her, alive and communicative. Where was God now, when her pain and her fear were intense? During the birth there was no bright gleam of an angel's wing, no encompassing light or peace beyond words.

For Mary, the whisper of angels came later when the shepherds arrived, praising God and telling her that the heavens rejoiced at the birth of her child. Mary had to believe what the shepherds told her, treasuring their words and pondering them in her heart. Christmas always comes to us as a rumour of love, whispered amidst the noise and frenzy, borne on the lips of improbable messengers. It is only through prayer, through gathering together all the scattered signs of hope that we see fragmented and dispersed in the world around us, that we come to experience God's love for ourselves. There is a delightful painting of the Adoration of the Shepherds by Gerrit Van Honthorst (1590-1656), which shows the shepherds as rugged men crowding around the manger in delight, and one can almost smell the nearness of them. They are a far cry from the angel Gabriel "with wings aflame" who was the messenger of the Annunciation. It was in Mary's openness to these others, to these strange visitors in a strange place, that she received God's reassurance. This was indeed the child who would bring peace on earth.

Luke tells us that the shepherds lived in the fields and took turns at guarding the sheep. They were terrified when the angels appeared. Elsewhere in Bethlehem, how many people slept soundly behind locked doors and knew neither the terror nor the ecstasy of the angels' song? Today, many of us live out of earshot of angels. Perhaps we need to look for the shepherds in our modern world and ask them what the angels are saying. They are unlikely to be people who live on exposed hillsides. They are more likely to live in corrugated iron shacks, crowded into ghettos and shanty towns. They do not have the power to break down our doors and make us listen, but they do have something to say to us about the urgent longing for peace on earth and goodwill toward those who enjoy God's favour. God's favour rests not on the rich and the powerful, but on the woman and her child in the stable and the shepherds in their field.

The wise men also heard the message, and they too have something to teach us. They set out with false expectations, hoping to find a king born into the trappings of worldly power. Perhaps they wouldn't have set out at all, if they had known what lay at the end of their journey. But there was something in them that was open to newness, and this enabled them to recognize ultimate significance in the child they encountered. So often, the minds of the rich are closed to the poor. The wise men had the appearance of wealth and power, but the landscape of their souls[1] was that of the open hillside where the shepherds lived, where angels appear and the glory and terror of God break through. T. S. Eliot's poem, *The Journey of the Magi*, describes the wise men's awakening:

> ... were we led all that way for
> Birth or Death? There was a Birth, certainly,
> We had evidence and no doubt. I had seen birth and death,
> But had thought they were different; this Birth was
> Hard and bitter agony for us, like Death, our death.

---

[1] "The landscape of the soul" is an expression used by Etty Hillesum, the Jewish writer and concentration camp victim.

We returned to our places, these Kingdoms,
But no longer at ease here, in the old dispensation,
With an alien people clutching their gods.
I should be glad of another death.

The nativity of Jesus was not the Christmas card scene peddled in a million shopping malls. It was a scene of hope in the depths of poverty and abandonment. Jesus was born on the periphery of life, not in the centre. There was no community to welcome him. There were only the shepherds, and later the wise men, who had to leave their ordered world and travel to the margins of society to find him. The nativity is repeated over and over again in our world today, but we have to pull back the curtains of our lives to see the star. We have to inhabit the rugged landscape of the soul if we are to hear the angels' song.

Increasingly we are being taught to believe that the poor have no right to procreate. In conditions of poverty and despair, the powers that be suggest that women should be prevented from having children. A baby born to a poor woman in a stable brings a different truth to the world. In times of war and famine and social crisis, birth rates tend to increase rather than decline. It is as if the birth of a child defies death. The birth of Mary's child was the ultimate act of defiance. It was the birth that will one day defeat death altogether. Until then, the nativity affirms the value of each and every human life, however poor, however unwanted in the world of men. When a child is born, whether in a stable or a ghetto or a refugee camp, somewhere the angels still sing. In the words of a well-known hymn,

Yet with the woes of sin and strife
the world has suffered long;
beneath the angels' strain have rolled
two thousand years of wrong;
and man, at war with man, hears not
the love-song which they bring:

61

O hush the noise, ye men of strife,
and hear the angels sing!

CHAPTER 5

Two Turtledoves and an Old Woman's Joy—Mary and her Baby at the Temple

And when the day came for them to be purified as laid down by the Law of Moses, they took him up to Jerusalem to present him to the Lord—observing what stands written in the Law of the Lord: *Every first-born male must be consecrated to the Lord*—and also to offer in sacrifice, in accordance with what is said in the Law of the Lord, *a pair of turtledoves or two young pigeons*. Now in Jerusalem there was a man named Simeon. He was an upright and devout man; he looked forward to Israel's comforting and the Holy Spirit rested on him. It had been revealed to him by the Holy Spirit that he would not see death until he had set eyes on the Christ of the Lord. Prompted by the Spirit he came to the Temple: and when the parents brought in the child Jesus to do for him what the Law required, he took him into his arms and blessed God; and he said:

> Now, Master, you can let your servant go in peace,
> just as you promised;
> because my eyes have seen the salvation
> which you have prepared for all the nations to see,
> a light to enlighten the pagans
> and the glory of your people Israel.

As the child's father and mother stood there wondering at the things that were being said about him, Simeon blessed them and said to Mary his mother, "You see this child: he is destined for the fall and for the rising of many in Israel, destined to be a sign that is rejected—and a sword will pierce your own soul too—so that the secret thoughts of many may be laid bare."

There was a prophetess also, Anna the daughter of Phanuel, of the tribe of Asher. She was well on in years. Her days of girlhood over, she had been married for seven years before becoming a widow. She was now eighty-four years old and never left the Temple, serving God night and day with fasting and prayer. She came by just at that moment and began to praise God; and she spoke of the child to all who looked forward to the deliverance of Jerusalem.

(Luke 2:22-38)

Mary went through ritual purification after childbirth. This confirms that in the eyes of God and of the world, her purity was not some bizarre physical condition which set her apart from other women. Like all women, Mary menstruated and she bled after childbirth. (Some early traditions suggest that she might have been a temple virgin until puberty, when menstruation would have made her ritually impure and she would have been barred from living in the temple.) Modern women have postnatal check-ups six weeks after giving birth. Indoctrinated as we are with the idea that we are a scientific society no longer trapped in a superstitious worldview, we overlook the fact that, as in Mary's time, we need some socially endorsed ritual that terminates the process of pregnancy and confirms that our bodies have returned to their normal functions. Today the obstetrician, often a man, performs this task. In Mary's time it was the priest. Women today still seek permission to re-enter society after childbirth, but the scientist has taken the place of the priest.

Women sometimes speak of being "churched," that is of going to church for the first time after giving birth, but today this private ritual finds no acknowledgement in the wider community. When the early Church ruled that menstruating women were to be admitted to worship, it was one of the rare occasions when the equality of the sexes promised in Christ was incorporated into Christian praxis, and I cannot believe that Christian women today would want it any other way. However, it is also true that the Church offers us very little space in which to acknowledge our gendered bodies and to incorporate the reality of those bodies into our spiritual lives. The rejection of ideas of ritual purity could have resulted in an acceptance of the body with all its discharges and cycles and functions, but instead Christianity has gone down the road of denial. We do not need purification because we are loathe to acknowledge that we have bodies at all, let alone bodies that leak and bleed. This denial affects both men and women, but in the processes of menstruation, pregnancy, lactation and the menopause women cannot deny their bodies without denying a substantial aspect of their own being. Among women ascetics in the early Christian tradition, the cessation of menstruation that accompanies malnourishment was seen as something positive, a step on the road to maleness that was regarded as the special privilege of the virgin woman. We might find echoes of this strange loathing of the female body in the modern problem of anorexia, which particularly affects pubescent girls. A Malawian woman theologian writes that when the missionaries tried to outlaw the rituals associated with the onset of menstruation, they met with such fierce resistance from Malawian women that instead they "christianized" these rituals by doing away with the rites of sexual initiation and incorporating them into the life of the Presbyterian Church, so that today the *chilangizo* ritual is still performed and valued by girls at puberty.[1] This is an interesting example of how Christianity can work to liberate women from sexual bondage, without creating a sense of shame and denial

---

[1] Isabel A. Phiri, *African Women in Religion and Culture—Chewa Women in the Nkhoma Synod of the Church of Central Africa, Presbyterian: A critical study from women's perspective*. PhD dissertation. University of Cape Town (1992)

about their bodies. Perhaps there needs to be some space in our worship for an acknowledgement and celebration of women's fertility, even although this strikes a chord of ancient terror in the patriarchal mind that has spent thousands of years resisting the fertility cults of the pagan world. When Mary went to the temple with her baby son, the visit signified many things, but one of them was her public acknowledgement of the physical processes of childbirth and fertility.

Luke's account of the Presentation also reminds us that Mary and Joseph were poor, despite the arguments of some Christians who say that as the son of a carpenter Jesus would have had a perfectly nice middle-class upbringing. Leviticus instructs that if a woman "cannot afford a lamb, she is to take two turtledoves or two young pigeons" (Lev. 12:8). This is the offering that Mary took to the temple. Having offered herself in her entirety to God, having conceived by the Holy Spirit and given birth to the Son of God, the Mother of God still approaches God with the offering of the poor in her hands. There is so much to learn from this. I referred earlier to the fear of pagan fertility rites. Despite the romanticization of goddess worship by some women today, we should be wary of any cult that holds up a great amoral force to redivinize the world. The powerful goddess is just as dangerous as the powerful god, because any image of God that is not rooted in the suffering and weakness of the poor is an idol that oppresses rather than liberates the human spirit. The central theme running through the Bible is in God's identification with the poor, personified both in Israel and in Mary and Jesus of Nazareth. So when Mary takes her child to the temple, she is the Great Mother of God but she is also the mother of the poor. Simeon speaks the language of salvation and glory, but he also speaks the language of rejection and pain. He identifies Mary's soul with that of Jesus, but it is in the piercing of her soul that Mary shares the work of salvation. When we see the image of God reflected in Mary, we see a woman who comes before God with her newborn baby and

66

two turtledoves.

Again and again, the Gospels invite us to look for Jesus among the poor, not in the sense of spiritual poverty by which Christians in the West so adeptly avert the challenge to our wealth, but in the concrete realities of poverty, in the symbols by which poverty expresses itself, making offerings out of meagre resources and weaving visions of redemption out of hunger and need. Mary had no lamb, but like Hannah before her, she consecrated her firstborn son to the Lord. Sylvia Plath's disturbing poem, "Mary's Song," woven around the domestic imagery of "the Sunday lamb," spells out starkly the cost of this consecration: "O golden child the world will kill and eat." Jesus was the shepherd and the lamb. At his birth, his mother welcomed the shepherds with whom he would one day identify himself. At the Presentation, she offered the Lamb of God to the Father although she had no money for a lamb. In some medieval paintings, Mary is depicted in priestly robes to indicate that in the offering of Jesus at the temple, she was performing a priestly function.

Simeon speaks of the laying bare of secret thoughts. What secret thoughts are laid bare when we contemplate this mother and her baby in the temple? Mary and Jesus were not confrontational, but as they lived out their ministry in the world, people found their masks stripped away. There was something in their goodness that was piercing and purifying, that exposed the darkest intentions and desires of the human heart as well as the most generous acts of love and devotion. The violent power of Herod, the cowardice of Peter, the treachery of Judas, the political opportunism of Pilate, all these would be laid bare. And it did not stop there. The Crusades, the genocide of indigenous peoples, the European wars of history, the fratricidal cataclysm of the Holocaust—while Mary's Son hangs dying on the cross of history, the powers of history ride out in his name to conquer and destroy so many children, so many mothers, and all the evils of the world are laid bare. Yet there is light as well as shadow. There is the light of Elizabeth's greeting to Mary and the anointing of Jesus' feet by the woman at Bethany. There is the light of Joseph's love, overcoming his reluctance to offer Mary and her child a home. There is the light that shines through all the long dark history of the Christian era, whenever men and women motivated by love of this crucified one quietly undergo their own loving crucifixions and die forgotten by the historical record, but still having added to the candlelight that has no blinding power but that casts a warm glow all the same. Sometimes today, it seems as if the most secret thoughts are those that are gentle and loving in intention. Our lusts and our violence and our failures are the public currency of the age. Where are the many whose secret loving thoughts must be laid bare if our world is to be healed and our broken communities restored?

The Gospel continues to lay bare secret thoughts, and if we would follow Jesus and Mary we must be sensitive to the secret worlds around us. There are secret longings and dreams and visions that need to be nurtured and brought to fruition. But there are also secret forces that corrupt and distort the fledgling visions of the human family, and these too must be laid bare. All the secret ambitions and lusts that pierce souls and reject the signs of redemption are laid bare in the presence of this Mother and Son, but so are the secret energies that give life to the oppressed and nurture dreams through long years of expectation.

Anna was an old woman who had spent years in prayer, waiting for deliverance. Anna is a symbol of women everywhere who yearn and fast, who live out their lives waiting for that deliverance that for some never comes at all, for others comes when they are old and near death. Anna is "woman." She is the one who waits throughout the history of unredeemed humanity for her deliverance, never losing faith, never losing the desire to speak out and to spread news of her hope and her vision. "She spoke of the child to all who looked forward to the deliverance of Jerusalem." How exasperated we sometimes become with the gossip of old women, with their endless repetition. How much we might discover if we learned to interpret their message, if we glimpsed their secret thoughts and began to cherish the unwritten history of small lives, of children and their mothers and grandmothers, of the long weary years of widowhood and prayer, of the prophetesses whose songs are not recorded and whose words are lost before they come to fulfilment. When Jesus was presented in the temple, a woman, a prophetess, was there to welcome him. God promises in Joel, "Your sons and daughters shall prophesy" (Joel 3:1). Why has the Church been so reluctant to recognize the significance of Anna's presence in the temple? What secret thoughts have made all the brothers of the Church beginning with Paul insist on the silence of women? Dare we hope that today, women are bringing to fruition the promise first glimpsed by Anna, that old and weary though we might be, after nearly two millennia of silence, fasting and praying we still have the capacity to glimpse the fragile sign of redemption and to praise God and to speak of what we have seen?

CHAPTER 6

Encountering Darkness—
Mary the Refugee

After they had left, the angel of the Lord appeared to Joseph in a dream and said, "Get up, take the child and his mother with you, and escape into Egypt, and stay there until I tell you, because Herod intends to search for the child and do away with him." So Joseph got up and, taking the child and his mother with him, left that night for Egypt, where he stayed until Herod was dead. This was to fulfil what the Lord had spoken through the prophet:

I called my son out of Egypt.

Herod was furious when he realised that he had been outwitted by the wise men, and in Bethlehem and its surrounding district he had all the male children killed who were two years old or under, reckoning by the date he had been careful to ask the wise men. It was then that the words spoken through the prophet Jeremiah were fulfilled:

A voice was heard in Ramah
sobbing and loudly lamenting:
it was Rachel weeping for her children,
refusing to be comforted
because they were no more.

(Matt. 2:13-23)

The first time we encounter Joseph in the Bible, we see him battling against the patriarchal impulse to disinherit Mary and her child. Now he has won his struggle, and he has become a loving and obedient participant in the drama of Jesus' childhood. But how can we begin to imagine the emotions that raged in Joseph and Mary as they fled into Egypt?

There are two episodes in the Gospel accounts of Mary's life that make one recoil from the reality of what is being suggested. They are the Flight into Egypt and the Crucifixion. The imagination seeks refuge in allegory and symbolism, considering every possibility but this: that the mother and child caught up in this drama are real human beings who love and suffer and plead with God not to let this happen, to take the cup away. And they are not the cursed of God but the blessed of God. How is this possible?

Contemplation is sometimes sold to us as a form of relaxation, an escape from the stresses of modern life. But Mary, the great contemplative in the Catholic tradition, suggests a different model of contemplation. If we would learn from her, we must let our minds travel with her into Egypt and to the foot of the cross, and we must allow the raw pain of her experience to strip our prayer of sentimentality and escapism. Yet what luxury it is, to make a journey of the mind in a quiet room with our eyes closed, while those who really journey in Mary's world, the refugee and the mother in torment, are reduced to a disquieting flicker on the television screen.

Rachel's grief is the lament that echoes in the conscience of the twentieth century. Now there can be no prayer whose peace is not disrupted by comfortless Rachel, there are no church walls thick enough or devotions pious enough to shut out our awareness of Rachel's children who are no more. Language struggles and finally breaks under the burden of truth. We cannot tell it like it is in our century, because we have words that tell of the hell of the wicked and the heaven of the good, but we have no words that tell of the hell of the innocent. This is the hell that Mary and Rachel and their children endured and endure today in a million different ways, as the imagination of power finds ever new ways to exercise its demonic will over the powerless.

Evil manifests itself in different ways. There is the evil that appears almost as a force without perpetrators, a vast system that holds humanity in its grip and has its own momentum, perhaps because it is the amalgam of all our individual greeds and cravings for power but it amounts to more than the sum of its parts. When these individual sins become institutionalized, it takes active resistance to change society. In today's world, the institutionalization of sin is apparent in the world's financial systems, in the arms trade and the commodities market, in the growing gulf between rich and poor, in the burgeoning climate of exploitation. We are all aware of this kind of corruption of society, but none of us feels responsible. With the collapse of communism, there is now no balancing act or moderating force in global politics. Capitalism has been unmasked for what it is and the Western democracies are sliding into extremes of greed and ruthlessness that leave many of us feeling appalled but helpless. There is a sense that it is everybody's problem and nobody's fault. It's just the way things are. This is the kind of amorphous evil that created the circumstances of the nativity, the evil of a self-perpetuating system that exists to service the dictates of power without regard for human welfare.

There is another kind of evil that is more instantly recognizable, and it unleashes itself upon us with terrifying force. This is the evil of the powerful individual, of Herod and Hitler and Stalin, of the murderer and the rapist, of all who tear apart the fragile hopes that knit together the human community. This is the evil that Mary and Joseph experienced when they were forced to flee from Herod.

There are many incidents in Jesus' life that stretch the contemporary imagination almost to breaking point, but the flight into

Egypt is not one of them. Indeed, if there is a single Christian motif that is appropriate to our age, then it is surely the image of this terrified family fleeing before Herod's army. But those nations that flaunt their Christian identity are least likely to recognize the family of Jesus in the plight of the refugee. Some of the poorest countries in Africa are host to the greatest numbers of refugees. In Malawi at the height of the Mozambican war, an estimated ten percent of the population were refugees. Zaire has opened its borders to hundreds of thousands fleeing from Rwanda. There is an excess of misery in Africa today, but there is also an abundance of love. The African tradition of hospitality means that there is space for the stranger in the poorest home, in the poorest nation, and this puts the wealthy nations of the world to shame. In our times, the holy family would still do better fleeing into Africa than into Europe or America. Jewish families desperately seeking refuge from Hitler were turned away at the borders of Europe and America and sent back to their deaths. Bosnian Muslims were denied entry to the rest of Europe when they too became the victims of genocide, although for forty years the European people had been saying "Never again." Rachel weeps and refuses to be comforted by the platitudes of civilized society. She knows better. We have not learned from Rachel's grief. There are so many holy families trapped face to face with Herod inside their national boundaries, while Western leaders meet in conference centres and discuss strategies for reducing immigration and protecting the prosperity of their citizens. The flight into Egypt finds space on our Christmas cards but it does not connect with the realities of our lives. It is decorative rather than scandalous, stripped of its power to judge, and therefore stripped ultimately of its power to call us out of our selfishness into loving vulnerability. Mary and her child are refused entry at our borders because they are outsiders and immigrants. They are outsiders to our world because they represent *Immanuel*, God with us, but God is the Outsider, the Other, and we learn to welcome him only when we recognize him in those who are unlike us. God is with us in the stranger and the alien, and to the extent that we barricade these people out of our lives, we barricade God out too.

When Mary fled into Egypt, she experienced the darkest side of history, the very opposite to the world of the *Magnificat*. Two thousand years later, we still wonder how long we must wait until the fulfilment of Mary's hope. Children still die and mothers still lament while the Herods play their power games and massacre the Innocents. In Europe alone, some seventy million people have died this century through war and persecution. How long until our world is not a battlefield but a playground where the laughter of children is heard on the wind? How long until we break down the borders that both trap us and divide us, and begin to build bridges that will link us and liberate us? And what is a border anyway, but a symbol that exists only in the minds of men? God did not create the world with national boundaries. It is easy to imagine a border, to create a division. But to build a bridge, we must sweat together and work together and begin each from our own side, with willing effort and communication so that slowly, slowly, inch by inch, we build a walkway between us. Today, the infection of nationalism proves no respecter of boundaries. It is a contagion that sweeps across the continent of Europe and raises spectres to haunt us. Leaders in the Western democracies know that appealing to the electorate's fear of immigrants is one of the most volatile and powerful weapons in their armoury of vote-winning tactics. In Europe and America, politicians are engaged in a dangerous flirtation with prejudice and fear, and they do not hear Rachel weeping for her children. They do not hear the voice of the mother who will not be comforted. Why are we so silent? Why do we not stand up and proclaim Mary's *Magnificat* on street corners and demand a world where Herod is put to flight so that children can live in peace?

So much is said today about a global sisterhood, but we women in the West have yet to learn the power of Mary's solidarity with her sisters in distress. Mary who hurried to share her joy with Elizabeth must also have shared Rachel's torment. John Donne wrote that "no man is an island." To mother is to experience that truth in the depth of one's being. The terror of mothering lies in the imperative to relate and to share. We cannot block out Rachel's grief. We can distract ourselves and harden our hearts and cling ever more desperately to our own precious children, but no woman is an island and when one is harmed, we all suffer. When a child dies, the brightness of life dims for us all. When one child goes hungry, the substance of our own world is diminished. When one child takes flight in terror, the security of all our lives is shaken. Women in the Western democracies have the power to change the world, if only we dare. We are co-participants in the politics of power. We elect the leaders who rule the world. Our failure to use our power in the service of life and not of death is written on the faces of the children of the world. Mary was safe in Egypt, for the time being. Her great ordeal was yet to come. But Mary suffered with Rachel and grieved with her, and if there was any comfort to be had, perhaps it was in remembering the *Magnificat* and in knowing that the baby at her breast was the mysterious fulfilment of that promise. Today, those of us who live in fragile safety also need to nurture the Christ among us by keeping the *Magnificat* before us, by knowing the purpose for which we have been spared, and the task to which we are called.

We must also be alive to the signs of hope, because perhaps despair is the greatest enemy of all, with the power to sap our energy and destroy our optimism so that we can no longer imagine or work for a better world. Despair has many guises, but the most insidious of all is the guise of the human being posing as the satisfied customer of life, the privileged individual who covers up his or her existential longing with the glossy smile of the consumer and colludes in the myth that this is the sum total of meaning and truth. This is the face that is turned away from life in despair, because it signifies the person who has abandoned hope and has surrendered herself to the fragmentation of being. The satisfied customer no longer looks for meaning, no longer rages against injustice and fights to be. She spends and she shops and she squanders herself on trivia, because the pain of the world is written too boldly on her television screen, and the hope of the world is a text within a text that must be studied and deciphered and understood, and there is no time for the quietude and watchfulness that such a task demands. Mary pondered things in her heart. Too often, we think that such pondering implies sweet submission and a willingness to be tossed this way and that in the storms of life without so much as a murmur of protest. But Mary is the woman of the Annunciation and the *Magnificat*, the wild brave woman of God. When Mary pondered in her heart what Herod had done, surely she felt gripped by holy rage, a rage that gave her the energy and the commitment to persevere and to turn her face again and again through life to those who would silence and destroy her? We must not be afraid of such holy rage. Conceived in hope and not in despair, holy rage is the birthing pain of the living commitment we need to change the world. It is the numbness of indifference that should terrify us, not the passion of hope.

In our world today no less than ever before, there are heroes as well as victims, and sometimes to be a victim is also to be a hero. We should not romanticize the pain of those who are overwhelmed by life, but nor should we be blind to the small acts of courage and hope that illumine our world and shine out of the darkest nights. We might never know the total of these acts of courage, because they go unobserved and unacknowledged by all but those closest to them, far from the glare of the television cameras and the soundbites of journalists. There is a well-known story of a reporter in the Congo who approached a group of nuns saying, "Anyone here speak English and been raped?" That is the kind of news we look for today. But what would happen instead if we were alert to the goodness and the gentleness of people, to the astonishing acts of generosity that inspire the human spirit to struggle and to survive through the very worst that one human being is capable of doing to another?

Confronted with the terror of Herod, Mary and Joseph faced the kind of appalling choice that faces too many people today: whether to flee from home and family and friends, possibly endangering those who stay even further by the very act of running away, or whether to wait helplessly behind flimsy doors for the bullet and the machete and the bomb. Mary and Joseph were already far from home in Bethlehem. They had already become people on the move. Now they took the risk of flight, but Mary clutched her child to her bosom and ensured that the incarnate Love of God would survive the horror of genocide. There are so many Marys, so many Josephs, in our world today, living in dependence on one another and listening for the voices of angels in the din of battle. The loving trust that emanates from this pilgrim family is a beacon of hope for all those who struggle for physical or spiritual survival in the wilderness. There has never been a darkness so great in history that the light did not manage to shine, however feebly, afterwards. There have always been people with the courage to nurture love and to keep it alive in times of desolation and abomination, so that when the horror ends new life can begin. These are the people who are the mothers of history and the mothers of God, for they keep the memory of God alive when the whole world seems ready to forget the meaning and purpose of its existence.

It cannot be said too often that for many people, the events described by Matthew are all too real. They do not need any great act of the imagination to picture the flight into Egypt and the massacre of Innocents. They have lived through it, or are living through it. But I suspect that for most people reading this book it is hard to imagine the reality of these other worlds that surround us and that are mediated to us with great immediacy but with so little substance. We are not immune to Rachel's lament and we know all too well that Herod still runs amok among the Innocents. The media bring us images of events that share our moment in history and make us aware of the complexity of the world we live in but can also make us feel like spectators in that world if we ourselves have comfortable lives. Our reality might seem better expressed in the commercial breaks than in the news broadcasts, and we may feel ourselves trapped in a make-believe world of consumerism and artifice with no way out. Perhaps we read this passage in Matthew with that same remoteness, wanting to feel more than we do, wanting to be less complacent, but not knowing what God is asking of us. We are bystanders and we feel helpless to influence the great events of our time.

Or is it a form of arrogance to want to do something momentous and decisive? Neither Herod nor Mary and Joseph could have achieved their aims alone. They were dependent upon others who were willing in small and seemingly insignificant ways to facilitate what they were doing. Herod could not single-handedly have killed the children of Bethlehem. He needed the co-operation of his army first of all, but he also needed the complicity of all those who looked away and pretended not to know. The Western democracies are deeply implicated in many of the crises that are pushing humanity toward the brink. How often do we choose not to know? How often does Herod rampage among the world's children in our name, wielding weapons that he has bought from our factories with money borrowed from our financial institutions, while we turn away and say it's none of our business, or decide to say nothing because we do not believe we can achieve anything? Such silence is not innocent. It becomes part of the canopy of darkness that shrouds the earth.

When Mary and Joseph travelled into Egypt, they would have been dependent on the kindness of strangers. They were exhausted and frightened. The smallest gesture of hostility or of welcome would have seemed significant. We all have the opportunity in many small ways to become part of the narrative of hope for those who suffer. Every day, we make our anonymous contribution to the world. We do not choose our time and place and the circumstances of our birth, but we do choose whether to be participants or spectators, whether to do what little we can or to do nothing at all. Herod needed people to do nothing. Mary and Joseph needed people to do a little to make their journey easier.

I have resisted giving this story an allegorical interpretation, but while we should not deny the reality of physical hardship and persecution that it entails, neither should we deny that it is also a story of faith. The literal interpretation does not exhaust its full significance. When we read of Mary's struggle we read not of her defeat but of her perseverance and faithfulness. We cannot enter into her world unless we allow her spirituality to infuse her story. We cannot understand her physical journey unless we also understand it as a spiritual journey.

We have seen the young girl who in the ecstasy of the Annunciation experienced the beginnings of God's life within her. We have seen her joy in the presence of Elizabeth, her celebration of God's love in the *Magnificat* and her vision of a new world of peace and justice, not in some future realm but here and now, already accomplished. Then we have witnessed the reality of her situation, the journey into darkness and fear, a journey to the heart of a world of injustice that is the Kingdom of the prince of this world, the antithesis of the Kingdom of God described in the *Magnificat*. In Mary's world the lowly were not exalted. Princes on their thrones appeared more powerful than ever before. The hungry had not been filled with good things but had been sent away into the desert, back into Egypt where so long ago God's people had toiled and not lost hope. Faithful to the vision of her people, Mary did not lose hope either. For the Christian, Mary is Mother of God and everything I say about her in this book has a Christian interpretation. But Mary is also the daughter of

Israel, and within the integrity of the Jewish tradition she represents something of the defiant courage of the people of God, who have wandered in the desert too long and been the victims of too many Herods, but who will not allow the holy name of the Lord to die in their midst. Like the Jewish people, Mary was stronger than those who sought to destroy her. She had that vision of the *Magnificat* always before her, and nothing could make her despair of its fulfilment. Her journey into Egypt was a journey into herself. It was a journey of discovery, revealing resources and strengths that had been dormant within her. She was discovering the measure of her faith and the extent of her courage. Mary, the young village girl, was becoming a woman full of grace.

It is trite and untrue to pretend that suffering is always creative. Rachel weeping for her children, refusing to be comforted, reminds us that much of the suffering in this world is senseless. There is no greater purpose and no ultimate fulfilment that justifies the murder of children. But it is also true that many of our most profound experiences of growing to maturity come not in the easy times but in the struggles. Suffering is not always creative but neither is it always destructive. It would be a very small God who could be trusted only when the going was good and life was easy. Mary was discovering the enormity and mystery of God's love, that radiant darkness that had enveloped her at the Annunciation and called her forward into the future in faith.

When God chose Mary, he did not choose her because she was submissive and meek and obedient. He chose her because she was a woman of extraordinary determination and perseverance, a woman of loving resistance and struggle. Her Son would learn by her example.

CHAPTER 7

Nurturing, Loving and Letting Go—Mary, Joseph and Jesus in Nazareth

When they had done everything the Law of the Lord required, they went back to Galilee, to their own town of Nazareth. Meanwhile the child grew to maturity, and he was filled with wisdom; and God's favour was with him.

(Luke 2:39-40)

Every year his parents used to go to Jerusalem for the feast of the Passover. When he was twelve years old, they went up for the feast as usual. When they were on their way home after the feast, the boy Jesus stayed behind in Jerusalem without his parents knowing it. They assumed he was with the caravan, and it was only after a day's journey that they went to look for him among their relations and acquaintances. When they failed to find him they went back to Jerusalem looking for him everywhere.

Three days later, they found him in the Temple, sitting among the doctors, listening to them, and asking them questions; and all those who heard him were astounded at his intelligence and his replies. They were overcome when they saw him, and his mother said to him, "My child, why have you done this to us? See how worried your father and I have been, looking for you." "Why were you looking for me?" he replied "Did you not know that I must be busy with my Father's affairs?" But they did not understand what he meant.

He then went down with them and came to Nazareth and lived under their authority. His mother stored up all these things in her heart. And Jesus increased in wisdom, in stature, and in favour with God and men.

(Luke 2:41-52)

So far, the picture we have of Mary's life is one of turmoil and hardship as a consequence of her assent to the divine will. By the time she came to settle in Nazareth with Joseph and her little son, she could have had few illusions about the nature of God's dealings with her. "Blessedness" did not mean a life of ease, and to find favour with God brought no guarantee of happiness. Nor is it helpful to suggest that Mary had some inner equilibrium that made her immune to the sufferings of Jesus' birth and infancy. Her prayerfulness and faith were not a barrier to keep pain at bay. Mary suffered in solidarity with all women who have suffered indignity and powerlessness.

But now we come to a new era in Mary's life. The Gospels tell us nothing about Jesus' childhood in Nazareth, so we have to use the few details that we already have as a doorway to the imagination. Again, we have to read meaning into silence, but this is in keeping with the Christian tradition. If great theological thinkers had not been able to tease the most profound significance out of that which is implicit but never clearly stated in the scriptures, we would not have the doctrine of the Trinity for a start, nor the creeds that have survived throughout most of Christian history.

In this chapter, I give free reign to the imagination and, as with much else in this book, it needs to be read more as an act of creative thinking than of scriptural exegesis. If some find greater truth in it, well and good, but its primary purpose is to stretch the imagination and explore the possibilities of Mary's domestic life.

There is an outward appearance of normality to Mary's life in Nazareth. During these years, the daily details of family life are sanctified by the relationship between Mary and Joseph and Jesus. Despite media images to the contrary, most people do live ordinary lives in the context of their cultures and times. We have the impression that we live in a disintegrating world, that everywhere there are starving children, bloody wars, embattled families, disconsolate and lonely people. While not denying the problems that surround us, we must be careful not to cultivate a culture of pessimism that is incapable of recognizing and celebrating the humdrum but blessed normality of everyday life.

In Western societies, we risk becoming so infected by consumerism and individualism that we crave constant novelty and stimulus, and we fail to value those quiet qualities of endurance and faithfulness that are the bedrock of our relationships with one another. Mary was open to newness and to difference. She did not cling to old ways of living or place too high a premium on tradition and social norms. But radical openness is something quite different from the inconsistency and whimsy that drive so many modern people to seek out constantly new experiences for their own sake. Mary must have longed for predictability and security, as she travelled first to Bethlehem and then to Egypt with Joseph and her baby. We can imagine the joy and thankfulness that she felt when at last it was possible to settle in one place and begin to experience family life. She had been on a spiritual and a physical journey with her sisters into the lonely birthing places of the poor, into the wilderness of the refugee. She had visited the world of women's struggle and pain, and she would do so again. But now she settled for a while in the world of the kitchen and the hearth, the world where women have for thousands of years woven webs of kinship and community. In a sense she had returned to the world she had left, and yet it was not a return. The woman who created a home in Nazareth was not the girl whom the angel had visited. We can never return to the past. Every day enlarges us, changes us, writes its newness into our life's narrative. We may revisit the places of our youth and reinhabit the family home, but we can never recreate the uniqueness of past lives and past experiences. Like Jeremiah, Mary had experienced the God who breaks and moulds the spirit. She had learned to yield and to sway with the currents of life, rooted in God but able to move so that the storms that buffeted her did not break her. All these insights and gifts Mary brought to Nazareth, to the home where she would teach Jesus the fundamental lessons of life. When the doctors in the temple marvelled at his intelligence, they were also marvelling at his mother's teaching and example, deeply rooted in her own faith and experience of life.

I think many of us who are happily married and live within the structures of the nuclear family want to create Mary in our own image during these domestic years. Feminists or not, we secretly believe that there is a "normal" way of being a woman and we want Mary to conform to the blueprint. In these days of reliable contraception, part of the normality of many women's lives is the reawakening of their sexuality, which by a combination of social prudery and the fear of pregnancy has been deeply suppressed in Western society. If we add to this the fact that Mary's virginity has been used to denigrate the sexually active woman and to foster a Christian culture that has failed to celebrate the goodness of human sexuality, there are many reasons why we may be pro-foundly resistant to the Catholic dogma of Mary's perpetual virginity. In these post-feminist, socially fragmented times, it testifies to the enduring power of the traditional family that many want to affirm the normality of the family in Nazareth, portraying Mary as sexually active, bearing more children, and living out the role of an ordinary wife and mother. There are several references in the New Testament to the brothers and sisters of Jesus (cf. Mark 3:31, Luke 8:19, Mark 6:1-3, Matt. 13:55, John 2:12). Even those who believe in the virgin birth often see no reason why Mary should have remained a virgin. The doctrine of her perpetual virginity can be interpreted as a piece of wish fulfilment on the part of celibate males who secretly wish that they too had been conceived without maternal carnality. The dichotomy between the whore and the virgin is perpetuated in the images of Eve and Mary or of Mary Magdalene and the Virgin Mary.

However, if the doctrine of Mary's virginity is accepted as revelation rather than rejected as sexual neurosis, then we must ask in what way this doctrine contributes to authentic human liberation. We must reject any teaching that claims to be revealed by God, but that has no saving potential for the human being who is asked to receive that doctrine and make it part of her life and her faith. But even when in good conscience we reject some part of the Church's teaching, we also need the humility to recognize that we might be wrong, that there may be aspects of the doctrine that we have failed to understand, or that the complexity of human need makes it impossible to know for sure what really is liberating. Moreover, what seems liberating to one person might be oppressive to another. There is no doubt that the doctrine of Mary's perpetual virginity has been oppressive for many Catholic women, but is that the only truth? Might there not be another interpretation or a new way of understanding that allows us not only to embrace the doctrine, but to use it to challenge those who oppress and denigrate women? In what follows, I approach this question from a number of different angles.

Sexual liberation is a new phenomenon for women, and its benefits are still enjoyed by a relatively small number of women who have easy access to contraception and abortion, who have enough autonomy in their relationships to exercise some control over their sex lives, and who have the means to provide for those children they decide to bring to birth. In the context of a contented life, good sex is the balm at the end of the day or the icing that holds the cake together. No wonder we want it for Mary too. But this picture is altogether too simple and too naive. It fails to take account of the many times when things literally fall apart even in the most loving relationships, when we are exhausted by the demands of little children or burdened by the commitments we take on, when we experience the boredom and lassitude that afflict all marriages from time to time, when sexuality is not healing balm but salt in the wound or a raging obsession. At its best, sex might have the power to transcend all human joys, but at its worst it has the power to destroy us. The Catholic Church's traditional attitude to sex is imbalanced not because it has exaggerated the destructive potential of sexuality, but because it has failed to acknowledge its compensating joyousness. Today, the attitude of secular society to religion has many similarities—the oppressive potential of religion is rightly identified, but the picture is false because it lacks a balancing sense of the liberating power of religion. Not the least of the lies put about by the consumer society is that sex is always good clean fun. Even before AIDS, the reality was much more complex than that. Sexuality is about hate as well as love, about anguish as well as joy. That is why perhaps it is the closest companion to religiosity in human experience. All this is true, even in the best of relationships. But what about the worst of relationships?

For many, many women and children, sexuality is not a joy but a torment, a violation that leaves them to pick up the tattered fragments of their being again and again, and to go through life clutching these broken pieces of themselves that will not fit together. Catholic women in Latin America and Asia write of Mary's virginity as an inspiring vision of bodily autonomy for those who have been violated and raped. In the wrong hands, Mary's virginity becomes a tool to punish even further those who are already sexual victims, but when those same abused women claim the right of interpretation, when they take the Church's doctrine as their own and mould it to fit the contours of their lives, virginity is no longer a weapon but a promise of healing and redemption. God loves women as they are, as embodied human beings represented by the virgin body of Mary. Mary's virginity promises restoration and wholeness to those who are broken apart by the brutality of sex. It is the kiss of God on wounded lips. All

88

women need that healing at times. Are there any who can say that they have never felt violated by sex? And if generally we experience sex in the context of a loving relationship as celebration and beauty, we do not need Mary to endorse that experience. We already have so much.

The message of the Incarnation is not for the rich but for the poor. It is not for those who already have in abundance, but for those who have nothing. Mary's virginity is not just purity and autonomy. It is also a form of poverty, a way of identifying with those who know the pain of hunger and of unsatisfied need. We know that Jesus was tempted in the desert, and that his temptation came in the form of the patriarchal lust for glory and power. Why then should we not imagine Mary's temptation during these years in Nazareth, as a struggle against the seductive powers of domesticity and a privatized life? These are the temptations women face, the temptations that allow us to buy out of responsibility for the public domain and close our minds to the outside world. Like the temptations that Jesus faced, they are not necessarily wrong in themselves, but they had the power to deflect both Mary and Jesus from the mission that God had prepared for them. For Jesus, the choice was between worldly power and the shame of the cross, between legitimate ambition and the poverty of the Kingdom. For Mary, the choice was between sexuality and children and the womanly commitments of family life, and the way of the desert, the way of the cross. She knew from the moment of his conception that Jesus was destined to walk this way with her, but the same would not be true of other children. One day, she would be called to leave everything and to take to the roads with her Son. Putting aside her natural family ties, she would become the Mother of the Church. The greatness of her task demanded purity of purpose and single-mindedness, but it also demanded that she be put to the test. Mary was not God's slave. At any moment, she was free to turn to Joseph, to reach out, to surrender herself to the world.

In the strange struggle of Mary's virginity we see the power of the Mother of God, the power of the virgin. Sara Maitland's novel, *Virgin Territory*, describes the struggle and the power of virginity. There are images of the forest, untouched and unexplored, but dark and brooding as well. There is the child Caro lost in her own wild darkness, refusing to be tamed. There is terror in the virgin because she cannot be controlled, she cannot be possessed by the world of men. Outwardly, the mother of Jesus was the village woman of Nazareth. Inwardly, she was the Mother of God who waited in darkness and expectation for the call that would lead her once more into the jungle, and we cannot quite domesticate her. Mary keeps breaking free of the walls that men build around her, the doctrines that seek to contain her. That too is the power of the virgin.

Mary was the new woman just as Jesus was the new man. They both belong within the new world that was initiated at the Annunciation and celebrated in the *Magnificat*, but that will only be fulfilled at the end of time. As creatures and spirits of the new world, Mary and Jesus lived as a promise and a beacon to all who would follow. They lived not in Paradise nor in Eden but in this temporal, fallen world and therefore they were buffeted and tormented by the injustices of life, but they were not part of the sinful order of domination, and nothing in their lives lends any justification to those who would perpetuate the old hierarchies between men and women.

Joseph loved Mary, but he belonged to the old way of being. He inherited the patriarchal lineage described by Matthew and Luke, and both remind us that that lineage was broken in Jesus: "Jacob was the father of Joseph the husband of Mary; of her was born Jesus who is called Christ" (Matt.1:16). "When he started to teach, Jesus was about thirty years old, being the son, as it was thought, of Joseph son of Heli . . ." (Luke 3:23). Mary was a new wineskin and Joseph was old wine. Traditional marriage would not have entailed the glorious union of equals described in the

Song of Songs, but the sinful hierarchy described in Genesis, of the woman yearning for her husband who would lord it over her. There is no reason not to accept the Catholic understanding that the brothers and sisters of Jesus were either Joseph's children by a previous marriage, or cousins. Anyone who has lived in Africa will know that such titles are used to denote a number of relationships in the extended family.

However, before going on I must add a proviso. I have already referred to Mary's Jewishness as belonging within the inheritance of the new world initiated in her, but I believe that this is an important point that any Christian writer today must be at pains to emphasize. When I associate Joseph with an old and unredeemed way of being, I am not suggesting that Judaism is representative of this old way, and Christianity of the new. Both Christianity and Judaism are historical religions that have offered people liberation and bondage, consolation and distress. Both have an inheritance that manifests sin and grace. Mary was Jewish. As the first woman of the new world, she did not bear the taint of the patriarchal inheritance. She was conceived without sin (and this is why I believe the doctrine of the Immaculate Conception is important), and she established a new paradigm for male/female relationships, but she retained her Jewish inheritance and she brought her son up in the Jewish religion. As a Christian, I believe that the possibility envisioned in Nazareth two thousand years ago will be brought to fullness in Christ, but within that fullness I also believe that the Jewish religion has its own fullness and its own unique way of journeying to the Kingdom. Like Mary, it is born baptized, born fit for the Kingdom of God. Just as the Christian Bible includes the Hebrew Scriptures, so the Kingdom of God includes the Jewish people, their identity and their religion. Joseph symbolizes the disempowerment of patriarchy whenever and wherever it is found, in every religion including Christianity, and in every race and nation. In the strange disjunction between Joseph and Mary's

Son, something is broken and something is restored, but our minds are clouded by history and we cannot yet see the significance of that truth in all its loving glory.

Joseph was the man chosen to be the earthly father of Jesus, and here again I think there is a wealth of meaning to be had if we contemplate the nature of his marriage to Mary, and the model of fatherhood that Jesus grew up with. Mary and Jesus were set on fire by the love of God and called to lives of holy passion. Mary knew that all generations would call her blessed. Jesus glimpsed the cosmic significance of his life. But Joseph was destined for obscurity and early retirement from the story of salvation. We hear nothing more of him after the finding in the temple when Jesus was twelve. Yet Joseph was entrusted with enormous responsibility, the responsibility not just of providing for and protecting Mary's child, but the responsibility of respecting Mary's calling and serving her in loving self-denial. Family life might be changing today, but it is not so long ago since the whole structure of the family revolved around the father's needs. He had the best chair in the house and the first helping at every meal. When he wanted to rest, the children were hushed, and when his rules were transgressed, the children were punished. I think this pattern probably prevails today in many homes. This is not the model of fatherhood that Jesus grew up with. From Joseph, Jesus learned how to be a man who can relate to women in loving equality, a man who can enjoy women's friendship and participate in their lives without being threatened by their sexuality or their difference. Abraham, Elkanah, David—biblical stories abound of men whose sexual desire and longing to sire children disrupted their lives. Joseph breaks this pattern and shows a different way of relating, a different model of marriage. He was also the first one whom Jesus called "*abba*," the one who would teach Jesus the possibilities of that word when used in the context of the loving relationship between father and child stripped of all its patriarchal connotations, all its claims to superiority and power. God chose the virgin to be his mother, spouse and daughter, but he chose the virgin's husband to be the earthly model of his fatherly love for Jesus.

Again, none of this is to devalue the importance of sex, but rather to suggest that perhaps those of us who live in cultures that are fixated by sex need to rediscover how to value non-sexual relationships more than we do. I suspect that for many women, genital sex is the last and possibly one of the less significant ways in which we express ourselves as sexual beings. Perhaps this is why women's sexuality has so terrified the men of the Church, because it is hard to draw lines around it and say exactly what it is, or where it begins and ends. The consummate sexual experience for women may not be intercourse at all but childbirth, and in this Mary shared in the sexual experience of every woman who has given birth and breastfed her baby. Virginity is not the same as asexuality. The most sublime and erotically charged relationships might be completely lacking in physical sex. To say that Mary and Joseph were celibate is not the same as saying that their relationship was asexual. People who choose celibacy sometimes speak of the energy and creativity that is unleashed, as their lives become focused on aspects of themselves other than their sexuality. Throughout Christian history, many women have found that the religious life releases them from the consuming demands of family life and liberates them for scholarship and social activity. So often, women are beguiled into elevating that which is trivial into positions of quite unjustifiable importance. When we yearn to put aside all the foolish distractions of women's lives to give our all to a project or a vision or a belief, we feel guilty and selfish. It is a wonderful patriarchal ruse that women's guilt should increase in direct proportion to the decrease in our servitude to male ambitions. When we feel guilty about clearing a space in our lives for those things that we believe are more important than the immediate demands which always confront us, we can I believe draw comfort from the example of Mary. Mary said no to everything that interfered with her great goal in life. Hers was a life that was ordered and directed, not according to some blueprint of normality (she was not a social conformist), but according to the inner harmony of a spirit that danced in perfect time to the music of God.

Yet that music has a plaintive note. Mary provided a home for her child and watched him grow during a childhood of relative peace and stability, but how could she ever forget Rachel's children? Sorrow had come to brood in Mary. It would not, could not, go away. Mary's song is the *Magnificat*. We know her Utopia, we have seen her dreams. But Mary knew that the world in which her little boy had found a precarious foothold was not the world of the *Magnificat*. She knew not just the daily anxieties of mothers' lives but the deeper, darker dread of loving too much, of being too vulnerable. To love so much and still let go, even to the point of death, that is the impossible, essential lesson of love. Only when we can love to that extreme are we free to love to the fullness of our being. I cannot imagine such love, but I see it expressed in Mary's life.

For Mary, as for so many women, the process of letting go began as Jesus approached adolescence. He had reached that age when children's worlds expand, and parental influence begins to diminish. For all mothers, these years of early adolescence entail allowing our children to become separate individuals, no longer dependent on us and no longer circumscribed within the worlds we define for them. It is a time of transition in motherhood, when we must learn new ways of relating to our children as we begin to know them as young adults, with their own ways of understanding the world that may be very different to our own. It is a time of bewilderment and perplexity, of discovery and change, and also of trust. For mothers who like to feel needed and who enjoy the dependent years of childhood, these adolescent years can be traumatic. For women who feel restricted by the demands of young children, adolescence can be a time of liberation and new horizons for the mother no less than for the child.

For Mary, the finding in the temple signalled a shift in her relationship with Jesus. It was an invitation to move beyond the nurturing days of childhood, into a new and independent role in her Son's ministry. Such a change necessitated reflection and prayer. At first, she did not understand what was being asked of her. In the solitude of her inner life, she would spend the next few years quietly assimilating the changes in Jesus and in her own calling. "His mother stored up all these things in her heart." Perhaps she felt that she had returned to the days before the Annunciation, when she glimpsed some greater purpose ahead of her, but had yet to discern what that purpose might be. She had served God faithfully in mothering his young Son. She had imparted her own faith to him, and now in the flowering of that faith she found herself challenged and made to redefine her role. Jesus was beginning to discover his mission. He recognized the primacy of his Father's claim on him. The last two verses give us a glimpse of the spiritual journey taking place in the home in Nazareth during the years between Jesus' adolescence and his public ministry, and Luke's imagery is suggestive of pregnancy. While the mother stores everything up inside herself, the child grows "in wisdom, in stature, and in favour with God and men." Mother and Son alike were exploring the mysterious terrain of faith, preparing themselves for the long journey ahead, waiting for God's invitation and his calling. In the intimacy of her home, Mary continued to nurture Jesus as once she had nurtured him in the intimacy of her body.

Significantly, this is the last we hear of Joseph. Whatever Mary had taught her Son about the circumstances of his conception, the twelve-year-old boy had discovered for himself something of the nature of his existence, and of the tenuousness of his links with Joseph. When Mary said, "See how worried your father and I have been," did she expect to be contradicted? It was natural that she should refer to Joseph as Jesus' father. She would not have humiliated Joseph publicly by calling him anything else, and besides, by his role in Jesus' life he had earned the title "father." But perhaps Mary was not altogether surprised by Jesus' reply: "Did you not know that I must be busy with my Father's affairs?" Jesus was indicating to her that he knew the nature of his calling, the mystery of his origins. Joseph was not the one he would continue to call father. The day would come when this loving and supportive father figure must step aside in order for Jesus to instigate a new model of fatherhood, a new relationship between humanity and God. It was his mother, not Joseph, who would play a definitive role in his future life. Jesus continued to live under parental authority—although now it became a question of willing submission rather than childhood dependency—but all the time the focus of revelation and divine action was shifting from the family group to the Mother and Son, the woman and the man who were called to reflect the image of God and to work together for the salvation of the world.

CHAPTER 8

Water, Wine and the Glory of God—Mary and Jesus at the Wedding at Cana

Three days later there was a wedding at Cana in Galilee. The mother of Jesus was there, and Jesus and his disciples had also been invited. When they ran out of wine, since the wine provided for the wedding was all finished, the mother of Jesus said to him, "They have no wine." Jesus said, "Woman, why turn to me? My hour has not come yet." His mother said to the servants, "Do whatever he tells you." There were six stone water jars standing there, meant for the ablutions that are customary among the Jews: each could hold twenty or thirty gallons. Jesus said to the servants, "Fill the jars with water," and they filled them to the brim. "Draw some out now," he told them, "and take it to the steward." They did this; the steward tasted the water, and it had turned into wine. Having no idea where it came from—only the servants who had drawn the water knew—the steward called the bridegroom and said, "People generally serve the best wine first, and keep the cheaper sort till the guests have had plenty to drink; but you have kept the best wine till now."

This was the first of the signs given by Jesus: it was given at Cana in Galilee. He let his glory be seen, and his disciples believed in him. After this he went down to Capernaum with his mother and the brothers, but they stayed there only a few days.

(John 2:1-12)

This passage has been puzzled over from the time of the Church Fathers, and the debate continues today. It has generally been interpreted to indicate some lack of understanding on Mary's part about the nature of Jesus' mission and of her relationship to him. His words to her, which translated more literally from the Greek are, "Woman, what have I to do with you?" have perplexed interpreters by what they see as the harshness of the rebuke. Sometimes they are taken to mean that Jesus is severing the mother/son relationship at the outset of his public ministry.

I referred in the Introduction to the contrast between popular devotion to Mary through the centuries, and the official doctrine of the Church. Although the latter has given Mary a place of prominence that Protestants believe is not justified on the biblical evidence alone, it has still generally been at pains to stress her subordination to Jesus, particularly in recent years. Pope John XXIII said, "The Madonna is not pleased when she is put above her Son." To read the description of the wedding at Cana in this light does indeed suggest something problematic in the relationship between Mary and Jesus. Perhaps it is reassuring to those who support the status quo, to discover that despite the powerful message of the infancy narratives, Mary is after all just a foolish woman who needs to be educated by a man. However, if we allow ourselves to imagine that at Cana Mary is in a position of authority and Jesus is the one who initially fails to understand the significance of the moment, the passage becomes pregnant with new meaning.

There is no birth narrative in John's Gospel, but at the beginning of Jesus' public ministry John describes an encounter between Mary and her Son that constitutes a birthing process, as Mary pushes Jesus into a role that he appears not to be ready to assume. To the best of my knowledge, the image of birth has not suggested itself to traditional interpreters of this text, but in Ivone Gebara and Maria Clara Bingemer's book, *Mary, Mother of God, Mother of the Poor*, they say of this passage: "Mary's faith begets and gives birth to the faith of the new messianic community."[1] It is the first time I have come across an interpretation that echoes my own understanding of the significance of John's account of the wedding at Cana. This confirms yet again that when women come to the scriptures, we often have shared insights that have eluded male interpreters.

Mary knew, with an intuition born of years of prayer and closeness to God, that a crucial moment had arrived, that God was once again prompting her to step into the unknown. She was not naive. She knew something of the cost involved in obeying God at moments such as these. Just as once she had pushed her baby from the nurturing protection of her own body into a hostile world, so now she was being asked to push him into the public domain, away from the private world she had shared with him for thirty years. The sword twisted in her soul. He had been baptized and he had called his first disciples, but now she had to break the maternal bond and surrender her Son to the world. She had to liberate him in order that he could become fully what God intended him to be.

Jesus was initially reluctant. Perhaps he knew something of the agony ahead. Did he hope that for just a little longer it might be possible to enjoy the old ways of living? Here we glimpse again the extent of Mary's focused obedience and faith. Her motherly love for her child cried out against what she was doing. She need not involve him. They could enjoy the wedding and go home together afterwards. Perhaps she could tell God that she had changed her mind. She was not, after all, willing to relinquish this man to serve some greater purpose.

Astonishingly, we must consider the possibility that once again, the history of the world hinged on Mary's decision. At this moment, perhaps Mary held the divinity of Christ in her hands.

[1] Ivone Gebara and Maria Clara Bingemer, *Mary, Mother of God, Mother of the Poor.* Tunbridge Wells: Burns & Oates (1989), p. 80

She had to make the final decision on behalf of the human race. Was this child grown to adulthood, this beloved son, to remain forever the son of Mary and of Adam, one who had come to earth as a broken promise and a thwarted hope, or did humanity have the courage to participate in making itself anew by accepting the offer of salvation? The gift had already been graciously offered and received when Mary agreed to become the mother of Jesus, but this gift remained hidden from history, hidden from the public gaze, until Mary indicated that the time had come for the gift to be revealed. Just as once God waited for Mary's "Yes," so now God waited again. It was Mary who must utter the word that would allow God's will to be played out in history, that would allow him to reveal his glory to the world. Mary was the human representative, and in the exercise of her free will all humankind decides whether or not to expose itself to the glory of God.

Perhaps Jesus knew what was happening, and rather than learning from her he was testing her. Then his response to her was not a rebuke but an opening into the future, a challenge to her, an acknowledgement of the significance of the moment. He was asking if she was willing to redefine her role in relation to him, if she was willing to become his co-worker and the mother of the Christ. His words to her must have been heavy with heartache and promise. He knew and she knew what their relationship had been, the tenderness and love, the intimacy of a shared secret, the togetherness in their experience of God. Now the wilderness lay ahead, and Jesus' mission depended on Mary's co-operation. She must go with him to the cross and beyond, in order for the Church to be born of her.

Mary accepted Jesus' challenge, and she did so, not by responding directly to him but by turning away from him and speaking to those who were present. In the very act of acceptance, she assumed her new role as mediator and co-worker, as the one who speaks to the world and commands obedience to the Son. His mother had become "*gynai*," woman, representative of all her sisters who had waited through history and who continue to wait today to become "woman" again—defined not in relation to their sons and husbands but recognized as co-equals with men in the Kingdom of God that has come and which is to come. From early times, theologians have detected a reference to Eve in the use of the word "woman." Elsewhere in John's Gospel, the Samaritan woman at the well and Mary Magdalene are referred to as "*gynai*" (John 4:21 and John 20:13), and Mary at the foot of the cross is called "*gynai*" by Jesus. It is a person called "woman" to whom Jesus first revealed himself. It is a person called "woman" who created the circumstances of his self-revelation at the wedding at Cana. It is a person called "woman" who became the Church, the mother of the Christian community, at the crucifixion, and it is a person called "woman" who was the first witness of the Resurrection in John's Gospel: "Jesus said, 'Woman, why are you weeping? Who are you looking for?'" (John 20:15). Jesus asked Mary, "Woman, what have I to do with you?" and if we would answer that question for ourselves, we must all become "*gynai*," women who weep and look for that which the world cannot give. "Woman" is a redeeming word that resounds back through all of history to Eve, catching up the whole community of believers into the motherly Kingdom of God. It is a Kingdom that is expressed in body and in spirit, a Kingdom on earth and in heaven, that was born bodily in Bethlehem and that was born again in the community of believers at Cana, when Jesus revealed his glory and his disciples believed.

The words "My hour has not yet come" are also suggestive of birth. When Mary was in Bethlehem, "the time came for her to have her child" (Luke 2:6). Just before the crucifixion, Jesus said to his disciples: "A woman in childbirth suffers, because her time has come" (John 16:21). The hour to which Jesus refers is taken to mean the crucifixion, but as I have said before, our experiences of birth and death are very close. In a sense, Mary was telling Jesus in Cana that his hour had indeed come, but Jesus was perhaps also asking Mary if she was willing to give birth to this event, to this new birth of all humanity. The mother who gives birth knows that she gives birth to one who must die. The shadow of death hovers over every image of birth, just as the hope of resurrection hovers over every image of death. Jesus' self-revelation in Cana was the beginning of the end, which was in itself another beginning.

"Do whatever he tells you," Mary told the servants, and we hear in her words a distant echo of her words to the angel in Luke: "Let what you have said be done to me." When humanity hears and obeys God's Word, God's presence is revealed. Jesus knew, from the way his mother spoke, that his hour had indeed come. Where once she had birthed him in water and blood, now she birthed him again in water and wine. Mary was both mother and priest. It was through her words that Jesus made an offering of himself in the transformation of water into wine, and he was revealed to his followers. He was born among them in a new way: "He let his glory be seen, and his disciples believed in him."

There is a sense in which the marriage at Cana represents the marriage between the Spirit and the Bride, between the Woman (Eve/Mary) and the Man (Adam/Christ), in whom the image of God is restored and the conflict between the sexes is healed. In one of the beautiful paradoxes of the Catholic faith, Mary has always been both Mother and Bride of Christ. The wedding at Cana is imbued with rich spiritual significance and there is much that the imagination can play with in this image of Christ and the Virgin Mary celebrating their mystical union at a wedding feast. But every time Mary is mentioned in the New Testament, we see the marriage of heaven and earth, the relevance of the body to the spirit, the relationship between the divine and the human. Mary represents humanity, and our awareness of the cosmic significance of the wedding at Cana should not distract us from the powerful human element that once again grounds the love of God in a tender concern for the poor. When Jesus let his glory be seen, it was in the context of an ordinary human situation, in response to his mother's expectation that he would help those in need.

Compared to other crises that would prompt miracles in Jesus' public ministry—the raising of Lazarus and Jairus' daughter, the healing of the blind and the lame—the fact that the wine had run out at a wedding was trivial. It suggests excess on the part of the guests. Surely the host had calculated how much they were likely to drink? How often do we withhold money from the poor with the excuse that they will only spend it on drink, conferring upon ourselves the right to pass judgment on their appetites? We should remember that Jesus' first miracle was of abundant and possibly even unwise giving. He provided wine for those who had already had more than enough. However symbolically we may interpret this in terms of the Eucharist, we should also pause to appreciate the human aspect of the story. When we live in societies where excess is a daily fact of life, we begin to associate abundance with guilt and self-indulgence. In poor communities, feasting is a rare and joyful occasion, and the extravagance of the celebration is in marked contrast to the austerity of everyday life. Mary and Jesus feasted and drank and danced at their friends' wedding, and when the wine ran out she persuaded him to provide more. I love to think that perhaps they were both tipsy when Jesus performed his first miracle. After all, this is the man of whom it was said, "Look, a glutton and a drunkard, a friend of tax collectors and sinners" (Luke 7:34).

John tells us that after the wedding Jesus went to Capernaum with his mother and the brothers, "but they stayed there only a few days." As we piece together Mary's role in Jesus' public ministry, it is hard to know from the Gospels whether she travelled with him or returned to Nazareth. I find it helpful to think of her doing both, spending time with Jesus on the road and then going home to visit her neighbours and family. However, what is clear is that after the wedding at Cana, Mary's role changed in relation to Jesus. She became his disciple and his travelling companion, and in so doing she provides inspiration for women beyond the domestic realm, participating in the events that shape the world.

In Mary, women's lives are put into perspective. Childbearing and motherhood are for the majority of women the focal point of adulthood up to a certain point, but these functions, however important and valuable they might be, are not the defining norms of a woman's personhood. There is a stage in life when many women, given the means to do so, enjoy being able to devote themselves to the care of their young children, but when our children no longer need us in that role, we must learn to redefine ourselves in social terms and to perform different tasks, to make a new contribution to the world. Sadly, society rarely offers older women such new beginnings, and the Church is more likely to offer us quasi-mothering roles such as visiting the sick and baking for the parish bazaar than to suggest dynamic new directions. If we look to Mary for a way of living, then we must not just look at the model of the young mother nurturing her baby or the sweet-faced virgin of Lourdes. We must also look at Mary in relation to her adult Son, and she is a very different person from the woman of popular iconography.

CHAPTER 9

Sharing the Ministry of Jesus—Mary becomes a Disciple

His mother and brothers now arrived and, standing outside, sent in a message asking for him. A crowd was sitting round him at the time the message was passed to him. "Your mother and brothers and sisters are outside asking for you." He replied, "Who are my mother and my brothers?" And looking round at those sitting in a circle about him, he said, "Here are my mother and brothers. Anyone who does the will of God, that person is my brother and sister and mother."

(Mark 3:31-5)

Now as he was speaking, a woman in the crowd raised her voice and said, "Happy the womb that bore you and the breasts you sucked!" But he replied, "Still happier those who hear the word of God and keep it!"

(Luke 11:27-8)

Jesus had begun his public ministry. The Kingdom of God was at hand. His disciples were ordinary men and women, called from ordinary lives to learn new ways of being. Mary had been called long ago, but now she too had to learn new ways of relating to her Son. How are women to be defined in the Kingdom of God? The answer, in Jesus' dealings with Mary in the above two passages, is that they are to be defined in exactly the same way as men.

As with the wedding at Cana, these passages have been read as evidence of Mary's all too human failings in her relationship with her Son. They can be interpreted in such a way that they signal Mary being put aside. She had fulfilled her function in relation to Jesus, and she was to have no special status among the disciples. However, this is a disturbing interpretation of God's dealings with Mary. Here is a woman who voluntarily agreed to be a central participant in the Incarnation, who in the most intimate possible way became caught up in and transformed by the mystery of the Word made flesh, who remained faithful to her calling through the most harrowing ordeals, who provided for Jesus a home in which he could learn, by her love and example, the key to his own mission and calling in life. What does it say about our idea of God, and of women in the eyes of God, if we believe that after all this, Jesus pushed Mary aside and refused her any special place in his life? This is a patriarchal image of a god who uses women for their bodies and then discards them, who treats them as something less than human. This contradicts what we know of God's dealings with women in the Old Testament, and of Jesus' relationships with women in the New Testament. We must, therefore, refuse this interpretation in favour of a deeper and more loving understanding of God's dealings with Mary.

Certainly, these passages indicate that the physical bond between Mary and Jesus had become insignificant. It no longer mattered that hers was the womb that bore him and the breasts that he suckled. What mattered was that Mary's faith had endured, that she was able to move alongside her Son in his public ministry and to perform an altogether new role in the wider community of disciples, as their example and their inspiration. Mary was to become the Mother of the infant Church. That meant she had to forsake the role of motherhood in order to become a mothering person, a person whose whole orientation and concern was for the common good, for the nurturing of relationships and ideas that would foster the sense of communality that was such a feature of the early Church.

When a woman's children are very young, she is consumed by their needs. It is hard to believe, during the early mothering years, that the physical bond with our children will ever be broken. They are dependent creatures who cry out to us for physical contact and nourishment, for affection and meaning conveyed through touch and caress, through the protective embrace and the warmth of our bodies. Years later, we may look at our grown-up children and find it hard to remember what that bodily relationship was like. We learn to encounter them as adults and to express our bonds with them in less tactile ways. The mother and baby live face to face, in a small world that struggles to accommodate wider perspectives. But if that mother-child relationship develops in a healthy and creative way, there will be a gradual shift so that eventually, mother and child are liberated from one another and face the world shoulder to shoulder, and the love that was once an intense bond between them becomes an example and a source of comfort for others. So it was with Mary and Jesus. That primal love between them remained as strong as it ever was, but it had to be expressed differently, to become inclusive rather than exclusive and open to a world of strangers. It became a love that did not set boundaries nor impose restrictions, but that strengthened and encouraged the other to do what must be done for God's Kingdom.

Mark says that Jesus' relatives "set out to take charge of him, convinced he was out of his mind" (Mark 3:21). The passage quoted above suggests that Mary was among those relatives, although it is hard to believe that after all she had experienced of Jesus she would have shared their doubts about his sanity. Mary had herself experienced the absurdity and folly of obeying God.

She knew that to respond to God meant behaving in ways that the world might find bizarre or anti-social. I think we need to reinterpret Mary's presence among Jesus' fretful relatives.

We have already seen at the wedding at Cana that Mary was sensitive and responsive to people's needs. She was a person who made connections between people. Years before, she had gone to visit her cousin Elizabeth to share the newness and mystery of their pregnancies. I find it helpful to imagine Mary visiting the extended family, persuading them to accept her Son's unusual ways, trying to share with them the vision that inspired him and that continued to inspire her. How many of us as mothers have found ourselves in such a role, mediating between family traditionalists and our offspring who opt for radically different lifestyles and values? Mary visited the family as a mediator, trying to explain the rumours that were filtering through about Jesus' behaviour. Mark tells us that he had already scandalized the community, eating with tax collectors and sinners and being accused of blasphemy. Mary evangelized the family. She told them the good news about her Son, and urged them to come and see for themselves. Hence, when the relatives arrived and asked to see him, Mary was with them as she is with all those who look for Jesus in bewilderment and questioning.

Mary is not demoted in these passages. She is given an equal place among the disciples and held up to them as an example. She had done the will of God. She had heard the word of God and kept it. For thirty years, she had loved Jesus, suffered with him and for him, and learned with him and from him. Now she took her place among the new disciples who would learn, as she had learned, the challenge and the joy of God's calling. In the community of equals that was the fledgling Church, nobody had preferential treatment. Mary had no special rights because of her blood ties with Jesus. Nor was her place in that community defined by her womanly roles of wife and mother. All were mothers, sisters and brothers. This is one of the few passages in the Bible that uses inclusive language. The new *Catechism of the Catholic Church* uses exclusive language. Women as well as men are described in terms of "brotherhood." Two thousand years ago, Jesus could suggest to men that they were mothers and sisters as well as brothers. That must have been an outrageous suggestion to the men of his time. How lovely if once in a while a priest looked out over his congregation and described them as the sisters and mothers of Christ! How often do those who seek to retain male power in the Church by arguing that the apostles were all men take seriously this insistence by Jesus, at the beginning of his public ministry, that gender was irrelevant with regard to discipleship?

Today, we live in an age when women often have many years of active life ahead of them when their children grow up. Society offers very few opportunities for older women to use their experience and learning in the wider community. In the Middle Ages, widowed women sometimes became abbesses and gained considerable influence in later life. Hildegard of Bingen became a travelling preacher and an abbess in her sixties, and remained active until her death at the age of eighty. Teresa of Avila experienced a blossoming of her spirituality and her administrative abilities in middle age. The Church today holds Mary up as a role model to mothers, but what model is offered to women who have outgrown the mothering role? As I said in the last chapter, the quasi-mothering role within the parish is often all that is available, and women with an abundance of energy and wisdom find themselves shrivelling rather than blossoming within the Church.

When we are urged to follow Mary, we should do just that. We should stride out in faith and courage, take our place among the brothers and sisters and mothers of Christ, and yes, among the fathers as well, but on our terms, not as men in disguise but as women. The Christian community will only reach maturity when women become fully participating members in that community, and when womanliness is equal to if distinct from manliness in the eyes of the Church. It is not our wombs and our breasts but our faith that counts.

CHAPTER 10

The Dying of the Light— the Mother of God at the Foot of the Cross

Near the cross of Jesus stood his mother and his mother's sister, Mary the wife of Clopas, and Mary of Magdala. Seeing his mother and the disciple he loved standing near her, Jesus said to his mother, "Woman, this is your son." Then to the disciple he said, "This is your mother." And from that moment the disciple made a place for in his home.

(John 19:25-7)

As a mother, I cannot imagine Mary's suffering at the foot of the cross. It is for those women who have been in that desolate place, in that Golgotha that has had too many names in our bloody human history, to grope their way toward articulating their experience. Ultimately, the mother at the foot of her child's cross occupies a space beyond language, as does the entire tableau at Calvary. We struggle toward meaning, but it is a struggle toward an abyss, and words are only flickering candles that reveal an ever greater darkness ahead.

Mary's relationship with Jesus was no longer based on motherhood but had become one based on discipleship and a community of equals, but Mary was still Jesus' mother. The motherly God of Isaiah says to her people: "Does a woman forget her baby at the breast, or fail to cherish the son of her womb?" (Isa. 49:15). Mary was not important to Jesus simply because she was his mother, but she could not fail to cherish the son of her womb, and her suffering at Calvary was the suffering of a mother. While theologians have been preoccupied with her presence at the crucifixion as a symbol of the Church and the New Israel, popular devotion has always recognized and identified with her human sorrow. The thirteenth century Franciscan, Jacopone da Todi, wrote a lament for Mary at the foot of the cross, part of which reads, "Son, white and ruddy, Son without compare, Son, on whom shall I rely? Son, have you also forsaken me? Son, white and fair, Son of the laughing face, Son, why has the world so despised thee?"[1] In the image of the *Mater Dolorosa*, in the Way of the Cross and the many hymns and liturgies and poems that focus on Mary at the crucifixion, in the figure of the *pietà*, popular Catholicism has retained a sense of Mary's humanity during the Passion, and this tradition continues today. A woman from El Salvador says:

> I often think of Mary: I suffered so much when they arrested my son. When I went to ask where he was, they said they didn't know. I searched and searched, but couldn't find him. Finally, his corpse appeared, his head in one place and his body in another. I fainted when I saw him. I thought of how the Blessed Virgin also suffered when they told her that her son had been arrested. Surely she went searching for him and later saw him die and buried him. That is why she understands my sorrow and helps me to go on.[2]

---

[1] Quoted in Marina Warner, *Alone of All Her Sex—the Myth and Cult of the Virgin Mary*. London: Picador (1990), p. 213

[2] Quoted in *Celebrating One World—A Resource Book on Liturgy and Social Justice*. London: CAFOD, St Thomas More Centre (1989), p. 95

Throughout the ages, Mary as Our Lady of Sorrows remains a constant motif in the faith of those who suffer and who find in her capacity for suffering a source of solidarity and solace. Mary on Calvary is both mother and companion of all who find themselves in that place where nobody ever chooses to stand. She is at the heart of grief and loss and betrayal, but that darkest moment in history is also the greatest moment of love and faith. In the midst of violence and horror, a Kingdom of gentleness and peace is born. As Mary watches her Son's agony, she finds herself once again reborn as a Mother. There were so many births and so many dyings in Mary's life, a constant dying to self in order to be born anew, as a young mother in Bethlehem, as a disciple at Cana, and now as the Mother of all humankind at Calvary. As once she gave God's child to the world, now he gives her to the Church. In the moment of death, the motherly Kingdom is born. The Mother of God becomes mother of the poor, mother of the devastated community that is represented at the cross by a group of women and one unnamed male disciple.

In John's description of the crucifixion, a new story is being written in which women emerge from the silence of the past to become named individuals and key participants. The story of "woman" is the story of the feminine face of God that has been turned toward the shadows and the night in the making of history. "Woman," symbol of darkness and passivity and mystery because she has for so long been voiceless, finds herself named and acknowledged at the crossroads of history. "Many who are first will be last, and the last first" (Mark 10:31). Yet astonishingly, these women around the cross have remained invisible to the men of the Church. Every time we hear that Jesus died alone and forsaken by his friends, we hear the voice of the male who believes that only the male presence really counts.

The only male disciple able to expose himself to the experience of the cross is not named. While women become real presences, known by name, the unnamed man becomes a symbol of all men who must learn to live within a motherly Church, taking Mary as their example and restoring women to their rightful place. This was a man who dared to love and be loved, a man who could express weakness and vulnerability by taking his place among grieving women without shame, without running away. Men are not given a place in history for being beloved. Fame and glory belong to brave soldiers and statesmen, to men of action. This disciple was surely brave, for did he not have the courage to stay when all the rest ran away? But in the community of believers, qualities of love and faithfulness count for more than bravery. Peter lacked bravery but he did not lack love. Judas was brave, but unable to accept forgiveness he was also ultimately unable to accept love, for forgiveness is the precondition of love. None of us can known in advance what we would do in a time of crisis, whether we would be like the women and the unnamed disciple and have the courage to remain true to our convictions and our loyalties, or whether like Peter and the rest we would deny everything and run away. What matters is that our love survives, that whether we stand firm or whether we are among those who return repentant and humiliated, we keep the possibility of love alive within us by remaining vulnerable, open to the one who suffers, the one in need.

The women at the foot of the cross were gathered on a dusty hillside in solidarity with one another. One of the women was Mary's sister. Always in Mary's life, when her faith was stretched to the utmost God gave her a friend. How often, when we pray in times of distress, do we look for the gentle miracle of companionship as the answer to prayer? Friendship does not decrease the weight of sadness nor does it change the intensity of grief, but perhaps it changes the quality of suffering. To suffer alone and forsaken even by God, to feel unloved and uncomforted, is to experience suffering as irredeemable and without hope. To suffer in solidarity and faith is to suffer no less, but it is to suffer differently. When Mary stood at the foot of the cross, her experience of suffering was absolute. Her sister chose to share that experience, not in the pretence that she could make it easier to bear, but in the knowledge that her presence counted for something. The old cliché that a burden shared is a burden halved is not true. Suffering is not a burden in the sense of being something we can choose to put down or give away or share. When we suffer, grief becomes the air we breathe, the liquid in our veins, the darkness on the face of the earth. To step into suffering beside another person does not diminish the darkness, but it can take away some of the loneliness and the terror of the unknown.

This is what Mary wanted to do for her Son. In being there, she tried to share his darkness. That forsakenness of spirit that made him cry out to God became her forsakenness, her abandonment. She need not have exposed herself to that. She could have run away, like the disciples. She could have stayed at home, praying behind closed doors, shutting out the bleak hillside and the bloodlust of the crowd. When we talk about contemplative prayer, we so often imagine a life closed off from the world. But Mary, the great contemplative, chose to be there in the midst of the violence, and her sister went with her. There was hatred around the cross that Friday, but there was also sisterly love, women bound together by courage and devotion as well as by grief. Whenever the powers of this world crucify the innocent, there are women who refuse to run away, who express their resistance in the courage of being there, of being quiet presences in the midst of chaos. The women at the foot of the cross symbolize all the women who refuse to hide, all the women who sorrow and mourn for children killed to satisfy the dictates of power.

In our individual lives, we all go through the anguish of bereavement and loss. Christians have often turned to the mother of Jesus for consolation in their times of trouble. But Mary is not just a motherly figure in a one-to-one relationship with the individual believer. She is the Mother of the Church, and therefore she tells us something about how we must behave as a community. At the Annunciation, Mary co-operated with God's word. She became a catalyst for change in the world by responding positively to God's initiative. At the wedding at Cana, Mary herself took the initiative. She saw a situation of need and she took action to ensure that the need was met. On Calvary, Mary recognized that the forces swirling around her were far beyond her control, and there was nothing she could do to avert this tragedy. But still, she chose to be present at the very centre of the darkness. There are times in this world when the Church experiences an annunciation, when God invites us as his people, his women (for we are all women in God's eyes), to respond to his invitation. There are also times when, like Mary at Cana, the Church is called to be watchful and sensitive to the needs of the world, and through prayer and active intervention to ensure that these needs are met, knowing that if we take the first step Christ will assist us, and his glory will be seen. But there are times when we know that we are helpless. We see the face of evil unmasked, and we recognize that a terrible cosmic battle is raging around us. What do we do? Today, many of us wonder if our world is on a *via dolorosa*. We sense crucifixion and fury ahead, and as we watch the faces of misery and poverty and war on our television screens, we know that for many, many of our fellow human beings, that reality has already arrived. There are those who join the crowd, shouting "Crucify him!" Sometimes they are the mobs who gather outside courtrooms and at scenes of crime, believing themselves able to judge, qualified to condemn, as they bray for blood and retribution. We should remember that Jesus was a common criminal. People felt righteous indignation when confronted by his blasphemies. They believed he deserved to die. But today, the crucifying mob is most powerfully represented by those who are far from the scene of any crime, far from the smell of sweat and blood and the cries of human voices raised in rage or grief. They are the financiers who cash in on the misery of the world from a distance, trading in arms and playing computer games with the world's wealth while children starve. They are the moguls of the media industry who create entertainment out of violence, gorging the public on a culture that is increasingly capable of reflecting only the dark side of human nature, but which does so in a way that makes us all bloodthirsty members of the crucifying crowd. We pay money to be nauseated. We are seduced by violence and the exploitation of others. Or perhaps like the disciples we are sick with fear and guilt. We love Jesus, and we cannot bear to expose ourselves to the stark cruelty of human nature. So we run away. We find some quiet, protected place in which to pray and sing hymns and escape from the rotten world. We think of him, far away on a hillside that we cannot bring ourselves to visit, and we tell ourselves that at least we are not involved. We are not like those in the crowd who demand blood.

But from the cross, Jesus tells us that Mary is our example. Mary neither joined the crowd nor ran away. She was there, remarkable in her perseverance and her love. She ensured that the flickering candle continued to cast its light in the abyss. This is the Church at its best, and although Christians often fail to emulate Mary, although there are many, many more of us who follow the instinct to flee or to join the crowd, in every age there are those who take Mary as their example, and become a faint and loving glow in the greatest darkness. When the genocide in Rwanda was at its peak in 1994, Catholic churches were scenes of some of the greatest slaughters, as people seeking sanctuary were hunted down. In that situation, the Church emulates her mother. She opens her heart to her children, even when she can do nothing but share in their agony.

If we always look at the cross in the light of the Resurrection, we may miss much of what it has to say to us. When we think of Mary at the crucifixion, we have to try to understand her bewilderment if we are to understand the greatness of her faith.

117

The cross was a moment of absolute brokenness. Her faith had been tested before—when the babies of Bethlehem were murdered, when Elizabeth's son was beheaded. But then her own Son had been spared, as a sign of hope for the world. Now it seemed that the darkness was too great even for him. The long journey into the unknown had in the end come to nothing. There was nothing but the whirlwind and the deafening silence of the One who had called her into its vortex. At Calvary, Mary contemplated futility. And even had she known of the Resurrection to come, what would that have mattered? Her Son, her beloved, was dying. What consolation would it have been to know that he would rise again in a body that she could not cling to or love in its nearness and intimacy? However much we might believe in the resurrection of the dead and the life of the world to come, that cannot compensate us for the loss of a loved one. We do not want a glorious, resurrected body. We want the familiar body with all its beloved imperfections and blemishes. We want the touch and the smell of that body beside us, the squeeze of a hand, the sharing of a smile and a loving caress. For Mary, Jesus was dying. The horizons of life had closed in on her, and there was nothing, nothing at all, beyond the dying.

But still Mary trusted God.

Mary at the foot of the cross represents the hope of those who continue to believe even when there is nothing left in heaven and on earth to make sense of their faith. She dares to love when Love itself is dying. In her heart, she keeps God alive although he is absent from all human awareness and reason. Kierkegaard calls her the "knight of faith," the lover who makes a leap into absurdity and paradox in order to experience a faith that goes beyond the power of the human mind to explain or to justify.

But Mary at the cross does not just represent humankind before God, she also represents God before humankind. What does the crucifixion mean for God the Father? On the cross, God the Son experiences the torment of death. Jesus, alone, forsaken, stripped of his human dignity and his awareness of the presence of God, incorporates into the Godhead the human experience of death and separation from God, which is the experience of sin. But God the Father, hearing the cry of the Son in his death throes, experiences the loss associated with death. We die because we live in a world darkened by sin, but we rage against death and suffer anguish when those close to us die, because we also live in a world enlightened by love and born every moment into the future by hope.

When we contemplate the death of Jesus, we contemplate God both as victim and as parent. We think not only of the innocent one who suffers death, but of the Father who watches. It is in Mary that we glimpse the exposed heart of God the Father, for Mary the Mother, alone of all humanity, has been invited into the broken heart of God at the moment of Jesus' death. How does the Father feel when the Son dies? Mary knows. What does it mean to watch helplessly as the beloved Son cries out in his forsakenness? Mary knows. She is the motherly love of God. God the Father is made present to the world in the Mother of God at the foot of the cross. Beyond the love and grief of the Father lies the unfathomable mystery of God. We cannot penetrate that mystery, nor can we come close to knowing the full meaning of the death of Jesus. But gazing at the Mother and the Son on Calvary, we begin to grasp the enormity of God's love and his pain. In the love poured out between Mary and Jesus, we begin to know the love poured out on the world that dark afternoon.

Mary is a real woman, surrounded by other women. She is also "woman," daughter of Zion, the feminine other who rectifies and thereby completes the image of God reflected in humanity. The God of patriarchy becomes the God who mothers all creation when the daughters of Zion become co-equal with the sons. The women and the beloved disciple stand at the foot of the cross as those righteous ones who keep watch and do not fall asleep, as those who discern the mystery of God's presence in the midst of

119

his most profound absence, as those who represent the possibility of keeping love alive in the depths of hatred and despair. Mary's loving presence on Calvary is pregnant with meaning and with promise. She is pregnant with the very image of God restored to humanity through the dying and rising of her Son.

CONCLUSION

Toward an Ending and a New Beginning

I choose to leave Mary at the end of John's Gospel, poised between death and new life, between desolation and fulfilment, between the cross and the birth of the community that is the Church, for in many ways that is where she remains for women today. This book has said much about the restoration of the male/female image of God through the restoration of women to their rightful place in society, but these propositions might seem laughable if we look at the Church and at the traditional Mary.

The Kingdom has come and is to come. Between Nazareth and Calvary, for thirty-three years in the history of the world, we glimpse through the Gospels an astonishing possibility that has not yet been brought to fruition. Written in an era when women were not accorded public status, by men who were in all probability already busy behind the scenes trying to circumscribe the role of women in the Christian community, nevertheless all the Gospels tell us that women were the first witnesses to the Resurrection. It is truly one of the mysteries of our faith that the Church has not yet seen fit to explore the significance of this. Why did the risen Jesus appear first to women? What does that tell us about the newborn community of Christ that we call the Church?

In Orthodox art, there are icons that show the dormition, or falling asleep, of the Virgin Mary. Her infant soul is cradled in the arms of Christ as he is cradled in her arms in pictures of his infancy. It is a beautiful image that completes the circle of Mary's life and perfects the image of God's mothering love. But the coming of the motherly Kingdom is a long and painful birthing process. We may turn away in despair and say that nothing in the history of the Church gives us hope that this is an institution capable of bringing to birth the restored humanity of women. Or we can consider ourselves among those privileged few who have been permitted to be present at the birth itself, when after nearly two thousand years of gestation the voice of women is being heard in the sacred vaults of the theological world. We are called to become midwives for one another and for our daughters. Do we dare to take up the challenge, or are we to remain silent, with our faces in shadow and our humanity forever consigned to the realm of night and passivity? I believe that this is a time of urgent but joyful struggle for the women of the Church, like the last stage in labour when the confusion and pain are intense and the mother's body is strained to breaking point, but the moment of birth is very close.

Who is Mary in relation to God the Father and God the Son? Many have associated her with the playful, feminine spirit of Wisdom who was with God in the beginning and was active in the creation of the world.[1] Is it possible that we see in this woman the very essence of the Holy Spirit, the dynamic being who communicates the love of the Father and the Son to the world and catches us up in the wonder of that love so that we become part of it, inseparable from it, forever belonging within it?

Mary the Spirit, the spirit of Mary, is both liberating and joyful,

---

[1] cf Proverbs 8:22-31

fertile and pure, in deepest sympathy with the laughter and tears, the dances and dirges of women's lives. The Church has distorted and abused her image in many ways but has never lost sight of her significance, her power and her centrality to the Christian faith. We must not betray her by abandoning her. Through Mary, we can learn once again to say *fiat* to God, even although we scandalize the community and cause priests to be struck dumb and find ourselves accused of drunkenness and waywardness. We have in our hands the silken skeins of scripture that weave intricate patterns of connectedness from Eve through Hannah and Elizabeth and Mary to ourselves and our daughters and our distant granddaughters.

> Happy the man who discovers wisdom,
>   the man who gains discernment:
> gaining her is more rewarding than silver,
>   more profitable than gold.
> She is beyond the price of pearls,
>   nothing you could covet is her equal.
> In her right hand is length of days;
>   in her left hand, riches and honour.
> Her ways are delightful ways,
>   her paths all lead to contentment.
> She is a tree of life for those who hold her fast,
>   those who cling to her live happy lives.
>
> (Prov. 3:13-20)

May God give us all the wisdom and discernment to nourish the tree of life and to mother our world to the fullness and beauty of his Kingdom. Mary, Mother of God and mother of the poor, pray for us.

Bibliography

Boff, Leonardo, *The Maternal Face of God—the Feminine and its Religious Expressions*. London: Collins (1989)

Gebara, Ivone and Bingemer, Maria Clara, *Mary, Mother of God, Mother of the Poor*. Tunbridge Wells: Burns & Oates (1989)

Graef, Hilda, *Mary—A History of Doctrine and Devotion*. Westminster, Maryland: Christian Classics; London: Sheed & Ward (1965)

Maeckelberghe, Else, *Desperately Seeking Mary—a Feminist Appropriation of a Traditional Christian Symbol*. Kampen: Kok Pharos (1994)

Maitland, Sara, *Virgin Territory*. London: Virago (1993)

Pirani, Alix (ed.), *The Absent Mother—Restoring the Goddess to Judaism and Christianity*. London: Mandala, HarperCollins (1991)

Ruether, Rosemary Radford, *Mary—the Feminine Face of the Church*. Philadelphia: Westminster Press (1977)

Warner, Marina, *Alone of All Her Sex—the Myth and the Cult of the Virgin Mary*. London: Picador (1990)

About the Author

Tina Beattie was born in 1955 in Lusaka, Zambia, and has lived most of her life in Africa—in Zambia, Kenya, and Zimbabwe. In Zimbabwe she published two children's fiction books that were recommended for use in schools there, and she is also the author of *The Boy with a Toucan in his Heart*, published in England under the name of Christina Bell. She became a Roman Catholic in 1987. After moving to England, she studied theology at Bristol University, and is currently engaged on a PhD thesis on Mariology and sexual difference in contemporary Catholicism. She is married with four children, aged from nine to seventeen.